Frau Guidos
4-17-98
Pembles

Overleaf: A young Cinnamon Pearl. Photo by Michael Gilroy.

Title page illustration: A
stained glass window by
Karen Eberle, depicting a pair
of Lutino Cockatiels, graces
the author's home.

Distributed in the UNITED STATES by T.F.H. Publications, Inc., One T.F.H. Plaza, Neptune City, NJ 07753; in CANADA to the Pet Trade by H & L Pet Supplies Inc., 27 Kingston Crescent, Kitchener, Ontario N2B 2T6; Rolf C. Hagen Ltd., 3225 Sartelon Street, Montreal 382 Quebec; in CANADA to the Book Trade by Macmillan of Canada (A Division of Canada Publishing Corporation), 164 Commander Boulevard, Agincourt, Ontario M1S 3C7; in ENGLAND by T.F.H. Publications Limited, Cliveden House/Priors Way/Bray, Maidenhead, Berkshire SL6 2HP, England; in AUSTRALIA AND THE SOUTH PACIFIC by T.F.H. (Australia) Pty. Ltd., Box 149, Brookvale 2100 N.S.W., Australia; in NEW ZEALAND by Ross Haines & Son, Ltd., 82 D Elizabeth Knox Place, Panmure, Auckland, New Zealand; in the PHILIPPINES by Bio-Research, 5 Lippay Street, San Lorenzo Village, Makati Rizal; in SOUTH AFRICA by Multipet Pty. Ltd., Box 235 New Germany, South Africa 3620. Published by T.F.H. Publications, Inc. Manufactured in the United States of America by T.F.H. Publications, Inc.

COCKATIELS!

PETS–BREEDING–SHOWING

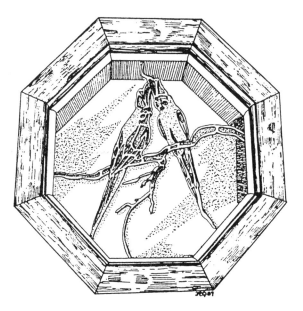

NANCY A. REED

Dr. Rainer R. Erhart,
Advisory Editor

Above: A pair of Lutino Cockatiels. Photo by Bill Parlee. **Facing page:** Two young Cinnamons. The "ticking" (light blotches) on the head of the bird on the left indicates that it carries the Pied gene (split for Pied). Photo by Michael Gilroy.

QUARRION QUATRAINS

Prink and preen, now, pretty Cockatiel,
Pet with popular appeal.
Proud as any popinjay
In lemon, orange, ashen gray.

Fan that crest high, little fop,
Feast on seeds and fill your crop.
Greet the day with cheery whistle,
Your antics dispel moods abyssal.

Nymphicus novae hollandiae,
Bird room or parlor, beautify.
A tribe from "outback" of Australia
Cockaded like cadet's regalia.

Gentle, affectionate psittacoid,
Your companionship is much enjoyed.
So strut and flutter, graceful 'tiel,
Most any breeder's heart you'll steal.

ANN SHERWOOD

ACKNOWLEDGMENTS

If you want to get technical, this book is the result of a "cast of hundreds." But it is obviously impossible to mention individually everyone who has somehow contributed to this endeavor. Also, to further shorten these acknowledgments, I will forgo naming all the contributors who will be credited in the text, for writing, photography, etc. Not meaning in any manner to minimize their contributions here, I hope I have already adequately conveyed my personal appreciation to these people.

However, there remain a few who I wish to purposely and publicly recognize and thank for their help and time–most especially Terry Stimpson, who has typed, retyped, and re-retyped for years. Without her, this text would have never become a legible reality.

I am also grateful for the help, support, and encouragement of three close friends: Mark Runnals, Jim Lamirande, and Bill Parlee. Thanks too to Karen Eberle and Tom Simon for their photographic-darkroom assistance.

Finally, my eternal appreciation to my family, who have accepted the fact that the birds come first: the corn on the cob in the refrigerator in January is not for *our* dinner, and family vacations have become an extinct "happening."

To those immediately involved or "behind the scenes," for what it is worth, I thank you all so *very sincerely*.

N.A.R.

Contents

Above: Comparison of a Normal male (above) with a Cinnamon male (below), photographed in daylight. Photo by Nancy A. Reed. **Facing Page:** A tame Lutino. Photo by Isabelle Francais.

INTRODUCTION

Why a Cockatiel?
Why not choose a Canary or a Budgie, a pair of finches, or lovebirds? Each has its purpose, as with breeds of dogs. A man wouldn't buy a bulldog if his aim were to hunt. So too, one shouldn't purchase a parrot if one wants a little something with a lot of song. Instead, choice of "breed" would be a Canary. A Cockatiel might learn to whistle the opening bars of "Clair de Lune," but would be a poor second to the Caruso of the bird world.

Or maybe you found a fancy antique cage at a sale that would be perfect hanging in your living room, with a pair of finches housed in it to complement the drapes. Finches do come in many colors and can live quite happily in a cage. But if you are more interested in hue rather than the birds' care, it would be more humane to use the cage as a planter. A Cockatiel would probably not accent your decor anyway, unless the theme was basic black.

But a curse upon anyone who uses a Cockatiel, or any bird, just for decoration! Birds *are* beautiful, but should be respected primarily as living creatures with vital needs. A wild bird can fill these needs by himself. A caged bird depends solely on your knowledge of his requirements. A dish of seed and a cup of water is *not* enough for any bird to thrive on.

Lovebirds, Budgies, and Cockatiels are all psittacines, i.e., members of the parrot family. They have far more in common with each other than with a Canary or a finch. These three parrot species are similar in diet, physical appearance, and personality. If you want a bird for companionship, one of these is your "breed."

But why a Cockatiel? Here the advantages of one over another of the three are mostly a matter of degree. Remember that each bird is as much an individual as people are. You can have five pet Cockatiels, and one will be the "talker," one the "ham," one the affectionate pet, etc. I shall only mention generalities here (and later hear of everyone's exceptions).

For one, I consider the warblings of a male Cockatiel (the female usually sticks to a single call note) less abrasive than the more persistent, harsh chirpings of a Budgie or a lovebird. When you consider a pet sitting on your shoulder and vocalizing close to your ear, or the calls being multiplied maybe fiftyfold in a breeding room, decide what you consider "joyful and exuberant song" and what's just plain noise. Once I heard from a person who thought the song of a Zebra Finch too noisy and wondered if a Cockatiel would be better. This is the type of person who would be happier with a Swedish ivy.

For a pet, a lovebird is by nature the least tame of the three, having a more nervous temperament. If you want a tame lovebird, hand-feeding as a baby is almost a must, unless you possess above-average patience. Budgies and Cockatiels are steadier subjects, and their inclination to mimic is far greater than a lovebird's.

As for lowest price and availability, the Budgie wins easily. But, when counting pennies, consider the fact that the Cockatiel averages the best longevity, an important factor when you become very attached to your little friend.

Cage size is another consideration. A pet Cockatiel, being larger, will appreciate a roomy cage more than a tame lovebird or Budgie will, but kept as a pet and allowed regular "outings," its home need not be a castle. However, curses again on anyone who loses interest or patience with his pet!— then a small (or large) cage will become a prison and an eventual coffin.

Above: An exquisitely marked Pearl hen seen from behind, in company with a Normal male Cockatiel. Photo by Nancy A. Reed. **Facing page:** A young Pearl male that was either lightly marked to begin with, or has already molted out much of his original pearling. Photo by Horst Bielfeld.

General Description

The Cockatiel is *Nymphicus hollandicus,* lone member of its genus as well as of the subfamily Nymphicinae, and one of the smallest cockatoos in the family Cactuidae, order Psittaciformes, class Aves—pretty fancy nomenclature for this rather small and somber-feathered bird from Australia. In its native land one would be more apt to hear the names Quarrion or Cockatoo Parrot in reference to this bird we call the Cockatiel (our name coming from the Portuguese word *cacatelho,* meaning "little cockatoo"). In short, this is a very popular cage bird by any name! Bearing the more streamlined body and long tail typical of the Australian parakeets, yet having the erectile crest of the cockatoos, it is considered a possible link between these two groups of parrots.

It inhabits the open country of Australia's interior: ground-feeding on seeding grasses, herbaceous plants, and fruits; and congregating near water. Nomadic in habit, flocks will follow the rainfall, which, when most plentiful in the spring (September through December), initiates their breeding season and assures a plentiful supply of food for their young nestlings in the hollows of trunks and limbs of trees. A curious trait has been observed in the wild: they avoid alighting on branches with foliage, preferring dead limbs where, as often as not, they perch lengthwise on the branch, rather than crosswise in typical bird fashion. I have observed my own birds occasionally taking this characteristic position on the larger perches in their flights.

The Cockatiels we see today have all been cage bred. Many generations have come and gone since their original ancestors were captured in the wild and exported to foreign countries. In 1939, Australia put a ban on any further exportation of their native birds. Had the Cockatiel not proven to be such an eager and generous breeder, fewer people would have the pleasure of their company today.

While the Latin word *hollandicus* was chosen in reference to New Holland, the old name for the Australian continent, I think it is also appropriately descriptive. A Cockie with his bright orange cheek patches does in fact look like a Dutch doll whose porcelain cheeks display identical markings. However, a verbal description of any bird is second-rate compared to a good photograph, so I shall be brief, preferring that you see for yourself.

The overall bird is approximately eleven to thirteen inches in length, its tapering tail comprising almost half of that measure. Its characteristic crest can be raised and lowered at will. Its feet are typical of all parrots, having two toes forward and two back, designed for climbing and grasping. Form follows function also in its hooked bill, which is strong and pointed for cracking hard seed coverings (and biting fingers in defense).

The original, wild-colored Cockatiels, which we call Normals, show sexually dimorphic markings as adult birds; i.e., males and females sport different colorations. Note the duller cheek patches of the female, the lack of a yellow mask, and the black-barred yellow lateral tail feathers. The depth of gray varies in individuals. Some almost approach black, which has caused a few breeders to believe they have a new "Black" mutation. These birds are only extremes of the original gray. This makes a very striking and handsome bird through contrast with the yellow, white, and orange accents.

Although the predominantly gray plumage of the Normal Cockatiel is hardly competition to the more colorful—and some downright gaudy—parrots, its endearing personality and prolific ways have caused extensive breeding of this species, which in turn has triggered mutations. These mutations have been a boon in increasing even further the popularity of the Cockatiel—voilà, some fancier clothes to match its super personality.

All right, enough on birds as pets. Many people start with a pet, find their interest expanding, and the natural progression is to try breeding. Of all the birds I have mentioned, the Zebra or the Society finch holds an edge on willingness to go to nest and the number of young produced. The other species are close seconds. However, the Cockatiel is fast becom-

Above: A pair of adult Pearl Cockatiels. No vestiges of the Pearl markings remain on the male's back. Photo by Nancy A. Reed.

Facing page: A Pearl youngster maturing in an aviary outdoors. Photo by Horst Bielfeld.

ing a close rival to the better known Canary and Budgie. Though more expensive, it is, in the long run, "more" bird. New and attractive mutations give a choice to those who consider the Normal Gray too plain.

Finally, why a Cockatiel? It is aesthetically a gracefully proportioned bird, and makes an intelligent and easily tamed pet. It is a good breeder, being a challenge to even the more experienced aviculturist interested in the genetics of mutations; and is longer lived than the more common cage-bird species.

The late Henry Bates and Robert Busenbark, who have contributed much to aviculture by writing about their extensive experiences in raising hundreds of species of birds, state in *Parrots and Related Birds* that "if we were suddenly denied the pleasure of all our birds except one, we would unhesitatingly choose a Cockatiel to be that one pet. . . . [They are the] best of all easily reared birds. . . . No bird can be more highly recommended than a Cockatiel." What more can I say?

Mutations
At this point, I'll just summarize the Cockatiel mutations. A later chapter will provide additional history and details of their inheritance.

PIED. In accordance with the Show Standard of the American Cockatiel Society (A.C.S.), a pleasing balance and symmetry of markings is ideal, with 75% yellow and 25% dark gray markings. Eventually it is our aim to breed Pieds that will be both consistently symmetrical in markings and heavily pied (predominantly yellow). Pied is a simple recessive mutation.

LUTINO. This striking mutation has been listed over the years under many names, including Albino, White, Primrose, and Ino. Coloration can vary from mostly white to mostly yellow, to more recent reports of some solid yellows.

All, of course, sport the orange cheek patch, which negates the term *Albino*. In this book I refer to any red-eyed white or yellow Cockatiel with cheek patches as Lutino, as has also become the policy of the American Cockatiel Society.

A bald spot behind the crest is a fault unique to this mutation, although in more recent years on the show bench a definite improvement is obvious. While heredity is considered the foremost factor, inadequate diet and overcrowding (resulting in plucking) can be contributory causes. Our aim must be to eliminate this unattractive trait, which varies in severity.

Lutino is a sex-linked mutation.

PEARL. This mutation is also a sex-linked mutation. With the degree of pearling varying greatly even within a clutch, it is our aim eventually to produce consistently heavy pearling, as well as males that will retain their pearl markings in adult plumage.

CINNAMON. This mutation's predominant feather color is silver to tan. On close inspection a Cinnamon's eyes are a medium brown, as opposed to the deep brown or black of Normals. This is another sex-linked mutation.

FALLOW AND SILVER. With these two mutations it can at first glance be somewhat difficult to distinguish one from the other. Both are simple recessives. Both have red eyes. The visible difference lies in plumage coloring: tan yellow vs. silver gray. The Fallow is far more prevalent in the U.S. at this time.

Irma Vowels of Florida is credited with the original Fallow hatching in 1971. As Fallows also existed in Europe as early as 1973, it is uncertain whether the same mutation occurred on two continents at about the same time, or if one stems from imports of split stock.

In 1974, David West of California received some Silvers from Europe. He states that while hatchings were numerous,

Above: A Cinnamon male in excellent condition. Photo by Horst Bielfeld.

Facing page: A Cinnamon Pearl Pied that has a clear face and nice crest, but the wing and tail flight feathers need conditioning. Photo by Horst Bielfeld.

Left: A nicely balanced (evenly marked) Pied that likely has a clear face (no gray feathers). A good show bird, provided its wing and tail feathers are cleaned beforehand. Photo by Michael Gilroy.

for five years fatalities among the young were 99% in the first twenty-four hours. In 1980, after five years of extensive experimentation without success, he finally chose to try indifference. Suddenly the birds began to produce. He has not found blindness to be a problem, though it was previously reported to be a fault of the Silver mutation in Europe.

WHITEFACE AND ALBINO. I first heard of the Whiteface mutation through the *Magazine* of England's Parrot Society (Nov. 1979). The bird was hatched in February 1979 and exhibited at a show in St. Neots. The bird was described as a cock with a clear white mask. He lacked any trace of yellow in the mask and body. There were no orange cheek patches. The head and shoulder patches were totally white. The body was gray, like a Normal.

This simple recessive mutation is in effect a "Blue" Cockatiel, lacking all lipochrome (yellow) pigmentation, preserving only melanin (gray). As an explanation of why a Blue mutation of the Cockatiel would not look blue visually, I quote the following from an article by Tony Barrett from the *American Cockatiel Society Bulletin* (Nov./Dec. 1979): "Unfortunately, cockatiels do not have a feather structure such that true greens or blues can be hoped for. I think that if a true green or blue cockatiel ever makes the scene, it will probably not be a color mutation in which melanin and lipochrome pigmentation is affected, but rather a mutation that has modified feather structure."

The Whiteface must have appeared in Europe at least two years previous to England's 1979 report. Dale Thompson took pictures of the Whiteface and Albino mutations on the European continent in the spring of 1980. Realizing that with luck it would take *at least two years* of breeding to produce an Albino from an initial Whiteface × Lutino cross, this may be another instance of the same mutation appearing coincidentally in two different areas.

As I recall reading in subsequent issues of the Parrot Society's magazine, the bird hatched in an Englishwoman's aviary. No mention was made whether she noticed the baby was covered with *white* down, in contrast to the usual yellow down of all other baby Cockatiels. This is visually very obvious, as the Whiteface and the Albino cannot show lipochrome pigmentation even in their "birthday suits"! Differentiation between a Whiteface and an Albino can also be made upon hatching: the former will have dark eyes, the Albino red.

The woman found the feathered bird to be unattractive because he lacked the colorful cheek patches and the usual yellow areas of a Normal. She did not know the genetic importance of this bird.

Here in the U.S. the name "Charcoal" was suggested as being more descriptive than Whiteface, because hens, of course, do not show a white mask. However, because Whiteface by this time was widespread in Europe, the American Cockatiel Society officially accepted this name, to avoid the confusion found in some Budgie and lovebird mutations in which the same mutation has different names on different continents.

While some might question the beauty of the Whiteface, compared to a Normal Cockatiel's coloration, this new mutation was the link to finally breeding a Cockatiel that lacks both lipochrome and melanin pigmentation. But this "Albino" is actually a *cross-mutation* (a Lutino Whiteface) and genetically is both sex-linked (Lutino) and simple recessive (Whiteface). Until an all-white bird occurs spontaneously, we do not have a *true* Albino mutation.

RUMORED MUTATIONS. Due to the Cockatiel's feather structure, we cannot expect the vast variety of colorful mutations that have been achieved in the lovebirds and the Budgerigar. Most likely we shall see more mutations in which markings will be the significant factor.

Here in the U.S. there has been much discussion over the "Lavender-wing." These birds were initially most prevalent in Florida, and in some shows have been given separate clas-

Left: A Pearl hen beginning her bath. Photo by Michael Gilroy.

Facing page: An evenly marked Pied Cockatiel with all clear flight feathers (no gray); on the show bench the bird would be penalized somewhat for a "dirty" face (gray feathers rather than yellow or white). Photo by Horst Bielfeld.

Below: A young Pied. Photo by Horst Bielfeld.

sification. However, the American Cockatiel Society is not inclined to give the bird official mutation status until its breeding is researched further. This bird is not to be confused with the Black-eyed White (or Bull's-eye), which has been proven to stem from a Pied heritage and represents a 100% pied bird (no gray).

At a distance the Lavender-wing looks like a Lutino, but on closer inspection the shoulder areas and lateral tail feathers appear "dirty"—or, more poetically stated, lavender hued. The eyes appear dark, as in a Normal.

Considering that A.C.S. asked that research be started in 1978, and no concrete response has resulted since, I personally tend to consider this "type" simply a Lutino variant. The eyes of a mature Lutino, especially if continually exposed to bright light, will appear very dark, if not black. Only when a ray of light passes through the pupil at a certain angle can the subtle red be noted. I have never heard that Lavender-wing birds *hatch* with black eyes.

I have judged approximately a dozen Lavender-wings on the show bench to date. Only one was appreciably different from the expected Lutino coloration. Upon returning home, I could look at some of my own Lutino *males* and see a tannish cast on the shoulders and the tail feathers, comparable to what I had seen at the shows.

I do not recall ever seeing a Lavender-wing hen—only cocks. Male Cockatiels in Normal and most mutations exhibit more melanin (dark factor) in adult plumage; perhaps even in Lutinos (theoretically lacking melanin pigmentation) a dilute melanin factor nonetheless becomes evident in some cocks. I've never seen an immature Lavender-wing. But I am not a geneticist, just an observer.

There is word of a "Clear-wing": Normal coloration except for white wing flights (maybe just a Pied?) And also an *all* orange bird (Wow!). I have also heard of Lutino birds with blue or yellow eyes.

There are also many reports of birds changing color or markings in the first molt (at four to six months). I have seen in California a "mutation" that molts from ordinary Cinnamon coloration into a Cinnamon-pied bird with the Cinnamon areas "marbled" (with isolated feathers on the back and the shoulders growing in white).

Often, isolated color changes (in a single specimen) may be a result of a metabolic problem; or the diet fed by the parents may affect the first coat of feathers, while the weaned youngster's choice of food affects the adult plumage. Apart from the reversion in coloration in the male Pearl Cockatiel, I have heard of one instance in other bird species of mutations changing color. In one pigeon mutation, the bird changes from dark to white. Interestingly, for show purposes every other feather is purposely plucked before the natural adult molt to give the bird a striking "checkerboard" effect: young dark feathers against adult white plumage.

Actually, I have heard of a lot of "funny" birds, especially when I was writing my "Rara Avis" ("rare bird") articles for the A.C.S. *Bulletin*. Sometimes I think we breeders are over-anxious to see a new mutation happen for us—like playing the lottery. Don't we just wish! In one instance a breeder was beside himself with excitement over his first hatch: all *green* babies! He invited a fellow breeder over to see this spectacular clutch. Alas, the fellow breeder saw Normal Gray babies. It turned out that the breeder was color blind.

I have read of the "Bordered" Cockatiel. In comparing the photos of the Bordered and the Pearl, I personally cannot detect an identifiable difference, other than the variation between an ordinary Pearl and a heavily marked Pearl (much like lightly Pied differs from heavily Pied). The written description of the Bordered seems to apply as well to the Pearl mutation, depending on which feather on the body you are examining. Some feathers are outlined in white or yellow; others are dark at the tips with white or yellow in the center of the feather. This was a European report, and I have not had any personal communication on the bird.

However, the main point about a mutation, despite its variability, is that it can be *reproduced*. If a variant cannot be

Left: A Pearl eating sunflower seeds. Photo by Michael Gilroy.

Facing page: A young Pearl male with a Pearl hen. Photo by Horst Bielfeld.

Below: Three Lutinos in "rough" feather that could be improved by regular misting with water. Photo by Horst Bielfeld.

repeated again after several generations of inbreeding, then one must consider the bird in question a sport (a singular oddity).

Trying to reproduce a characteristic entails inbreeding father × daughter, mother × son, or sister × brother. If for some reason such inbreeding is impossible, one should use *pure* (not split) Normal stock to outcross with, and then inbreed. Using other mutations, or splits thereof, will only confuse, delay, or mask the appearance of the genetic factors one is trying to establish.

Unfortunately, it is becoming more difficult to find pure Normal Gray stock. It would be wise if we had, as a storehouse, a few breeders perpetuating pure stock, remembering especially that a simple recessive factor can be carried for many generations without showing up. Commercially imported birds carry no pedigrees.

CROSS-MUTATIONS. Then there are "all the colors in between." Crosses of Lutino and Pearl, Pied and Pearl, Cinnamon and Pearl, Cinnamon and Pied, Cinnamon, Pied, and Pearl, etc., can prove most attractive, giving breeders a further wealth of possibilities to work with. But these are not in themselves "new" mutations. They are cross-mutations (two or more mutations visible on one bird).

To purposely breed for these cross-mutations entails some knowledge of genetics, obviously, as things become complex. "Starting from scratch," it takes two generations to achieve a double cross-mutation. (First year: breeding to get a Normal split for two mutations; second year: breeding the doubly split mutation to a suitable mutation.) In the past few years, many who have purchased imported birds have been pleasantly surprised to find a cross-mutation turn up in a clutch. Obviously some of these imported birds are harboring two factors and *by chance* were mated to suitable mates.

For instance, a novice may take, say, a Pied male crossed to a Pearl hen and, bingo, expect Pied Pearls. What a disappointment when all the young appear Normal! But these visually Normal babies are of more value if it is realized that all the hens are split for Pied, and all males are split for Pearl and Pied. It is from these double split Normal males that the Pied Pearl may possibly be produced the following season when mated to a Pied, Pied Pearl, or Pearl /Pied (Pearl split for Pied) hen.

And then we have triple, quadruple, *ad infinitum* cross-mutations! Again, these cross-mutations can be quite beautiful, but know what you are doing!

Behaviors

I would like to touch briefly on various things I have noticed that are typical of the Cockatiel. I have occasionally had frantic calls saying, "Oh, Help! My bird did such and so! Is he sick?" Often, what has taken place is just a mannerism peculiar to the Cockie and others of the parrot family, and no cause for alarm.

Hearing a bird sneeze can automatically trigger thoughts of pneumonia, etc. However, a Cockatiel occasionally will purposely stick a claw in his nostril, inducing a sneeze. Unless there is a discharge, this apparently is normal and natural, a bird's answer to an Englishman's snuff. I cannot answer the why of the action, but only that it is a fact of life with the bird.

Cockatiels seem big on catnaps. They are either active or not, and when not, they snooze. Unless the bird is fluffed-up, or will not respond to a "Hey, you there!" or a rap on the cage, or is huddled in a corner, one should postpone panic.

Also a bird may yawn wide, stretching and rotating his neck. This is most often seen on parent birds that just want to stretch those muscles that are being contracted constantly in feeding young. If the bird does not seem to be trying to regurgitate, again no problem.

Once a woman called me and said, "Help! There is something wrong with my bird's ears! He shakes his head when I talk to him!" At the time I was unaware of this mannerism,

Above: A Lutino in "tight" feather, i.e., in good condition. Photo by Ron & Val Moat.

Facing page: A Silver male. The red eyes are not apparent in this photograph by Horst Bielfeld.

but have observed it since. Occasionally, and especially with sounds of certain pitches, a bird will shake his head as if irritated by the sound.

It is also common for Cockatiels (and cockatoos) to hiss like snakes when afraid or angry (usually observed with untamed birds, parents, and especially young in the nest). This will sometimes be accompanied by rocking back and forth. It is a defensive gesture to keep you at bay.

Cockies are not keen bathers. They will wade in a pan of water, dipping their heads, but usually the tummy is all that gets wet. This is most often observed when parents have eggs in the nest. The moisture from the birds' feathers softens the shells, which facilitates hatching.

Most birds learn to appreciate an occasional shower. They will first raise one wing to expose the under feathers, then the other, while ruffling the body feathers and fanning the tail flights.

Many Cockatiels dislike change, both in diet and in surroundings. A tame baby may sulk for days in his new home until he adjusts. A sick bird (noncontagious) may respond better to treatment in his usual cage or flight, instead of being upset further by a change and separated from mate or companions.

Although a psittacine, the Cockatiel does not generally utilize his foot as a hand for holding his food, as do many hookbills. And when he occasionally does, he lacks the dexterity that other parrots display.

Another mannerism is the stretching out and back of one wing and at the same time the leg under it. This is typical of all birds, and over the years I have found it to be a sign of well-being. When nursing a sick bird, once I see him perform this ritual I know he most probably is going to be fine.

Cockatiels are long lived, although not to the same extent as their larger parrot relatives. Mrs. Rose McManamon recorded her pet's lifespan at twenty-three years, four months, and twenty days. Marie Olssen's pet, Bobbi, was born in July 1950, and died in July 1985, a few days short of his thirty-eighth birthday. These are exceptions, but certainly a bird of fifteen or so would not be unusual.

Cockatiels are hardy birds. They can withstand winter weather but should have a dry, draftfree shelter in which to huddle, and plenty of food available to maintain body heat. They are peaceful birds and may even be housed with finches. Grass-Parakeets are compatible with them; Bourke's being the best, Redrumps sometimes proving a bit too aggressive. Always keep close watch when new birds are introduced to a flight, as chances are, if there is any harassing, the poor Cockatiel will be on the receiving end and will seldom fight back.

Purchasing

A reliable pet shop is usually the nearest source for someone who is just starting with birds, does not subscribe to bird magazines, or is not a member of a local club. When buying a pair for breeding, I prefer to contact a reputable breeder. This is not a slight against my good friends who run the local shop, but simply the fact that they will usually not know the genetic background of the bird. If you want to breed them, this is important. A breeder likes to sell his best birds to people he knows will recognize and utilize their potential.

As most breeders set their birds up for breeding in midwinter and early spring, summer and fall are therefore the best times for purchasing birds from either a breeder or a pet shop. At this time there are more birds to choose from: they will be young (best for pets) and can be sexed fairly accurately. Be sure to inquire what diet the birds are used to. Individuals often have likes and dislikes, and if you are aware of these, this will help the bird adjust more easily to its new home.

Adult Cinnamon male Cockatiels. Photo by Nancy A. Reed.

Adult Normal hen. Photo by Nancy A. Reed.

CAGES, FLIGHTS, AND EQUIPMENT

Cages

Housing your Cockatiel can prove more expensive than the bird itself—be it a ready-made cage or materials for building a larger cage yourself. But a well-made cage or flight will be worth the expense in time, as it will not have to be replaced over the years.

Do not purchase cages made of wood or bamboo—in other words, destructible cages. Cockatiels are parrots, and enjoy a good chew as much as a teething puppy. Also, if the wires are painted, make sure the paint is leadfree, as fortunately most is nowadays. (Beware of a painted antique cage—better to strip all old paint off and start anew.)

Birds themselves are clean, but flying feathers and empty seed husks can be frustrating to the housekeeper. Many cages are equipped with glass or plastic panels around the bottom of the cage's sides; also, a drawerlike tray is most practical for cleaning. Seed cups that can be serviced from outside the cage are convenient, as one does not have to disturb an untamed bird or a breeding pair by reaching into the cage to refill seed hoppers and water fonts. A cage with horizontal bars is ideal (although not a necessity), as the Cockatiel can then climb the sides as on a ladder.

For a tame pet, the size of the cage can be minimal if the bird is allowed out daily to fly. By "minimal," I mean a cage that can accommodate the sixteen-inch wingspan of the bird as he holds onto the bars of the cage and flaps his wings vigorously (which he'll do when in need of exercise). This also means not too many toys or perches to hamper his actions.

Too small a cage can raise havoc with the bird's feathers as he climbs about—especially those beautiful, long tail flights. He can end up looking like a stubby bird with an old paint brush in tow. Don't place perches too close to the sides of the cage; allow him to sit with no feathers touching the wires.

In short, I would recommend a durable metal cage at least two feet in length; two or, at the most, three perches; preferably no fancy filigree; and, very importantly, one designed for ease in feeding and cleaning. A cage that is easy to clean is more apt to be *kept* clean.

Flights

If one has the space, a flight is the ideal arrangement. A "flight" is either a walk-in enclosure or a very large cage where a bird must fly from perch to perch, not hop or climb. Although there are excellent prefabricated flights available commercially, this is usually a do-it-yourself job. It will not be as "showy" a housing as a ready-made cage, but the bird couldn't care less, and it will probably not be situated in the living room anyway.

If you lack space in the house, you might consider the yard. With a little ingenuity (and money) an attractive structure can be designed for a garden setting. With less imagination (and fewer pennies), one can produce an equally adequate flight in a less conspicuous spot. The birds do not care about the frills, but can develop into strong, robust specimens in an outdoor environment. However, there are the additional hazards of rodents, cats, dogs, cold, damp weather, and the possibility of contracting diseases and parasites from the wild birds. I consider the indoor flights safer, but mostly because of the unpredictable New England climate where I live. If we could move South . . . (dream, dream, dream)!

The easiest and most economical materials for construction are wood supports (although a metal framework is ideal) with welded wire or hardware cloth. I prefer the half-inch by one- or two-inch 16-gauge welded galvanized wire. This will contain even the finches. Some use one-inch by one- or two-inch

Above: Cinnamon hen. Photo by Nancy A. Reed. **Facing page, above:** A Pearl and a Pied. Photo by Isabelle Francais. **Below:** Two Pearls enjoying a dish of various foods. Photo by Michael Gilroy.

mesh, which is also suitable for Cockatiels, but it does allow for birds' heads to pass through openings, and thus an occasional injury or fatality.

Recently there have been reports of bird fatalities due to a hot-dip process applied to new wire. Scrub and rinse the mesh thoroughly with vinegar before your birds are put into the new flight. Also, when snipping the wire, be sure to clip all ends close to the nearest joint. Too many birds have seriously injured themselves, even to the extreme of losing a leg, because a leg band became caught on a long wire end (or a small twig stub of a natural perch).

Smaller flights can be constructed without additional supports by simply cutting the wire cloth and using metal C-clips clamped on with special pliers (poultry suppliers will be familiar with this tool). On any opening into the cage (door, entry into nest box, or around feeding area), one should use a metal file (or easier yet, a grinding wheel on an electric drill) to smooth off any sharp nibs left from cutting the wires. This will eliminate the likelihood of scratches on the birds and yourself, or annoying snags on your clothes.

For a homemade cage or small flight, a tray made of galvanized sheet metal or aluminum can be custom-made by a tinsmith (remember to measure at least one-half inch smaller than the cage's length so that the tray will slide easily). When initially determining the measurements of your cage, you would be wise to design it so that newspaper (if you will be using it for a floor covering) will not have to be cut or folded. This will omit an extra task at cleaning time.

Perches

Perches are a very important part of the bird's life, as 99% of his time is spent on them. Manufactured cages are usually supplied with wooden dowels or plastic perches. These are neater in appearance and easier to clean but are not as good for the bird's feet as would be a tree branch, which varies in circumference. If dowels are preferred, use rods of varying widths in the cage (⅝" or ¾" diameter is best for the birds' favorite perch). The foot should not be subjected to an unvarying grasp. This is why a natural branch is ideal, giving the feet a variety of grips. Also, the birds will welcome the opportunity to chew on these (seeing as we have caged them in an indestructible housing). This is good for their beaks and also beneficial nutritionally. Soft-barked, nonpoisonous trees such as willow, sassafras, and apple are particularly relished. When the branches are either chewed to the limit or soiled, they are easily replaced with fresh ones. These branches (ideally averaging one-half inch to one inch in diameter) are situated about one foot from the sides and top of flight so that no tail or crest feathers are touching the wires. It is best to use a minimum of perches, to allow the bird freedom of movement. Positions should vary; however, the highest perches are usually preferred by the birds. The sandpaper covering sold for cage perches are unnecessary and detrimental to the bird's feet.

An occasional bird will suffer from overgrown claws and need frequent clippings. Perches of larger diameter (¾″ to 1¼″ may help, as the claw tips will be constantly in contact with the wood and therefore worn down at a faster rate.

Floor Coverings
In an outside flight, a natural earth floor is already present, but it creates easy access for burrowing rodents if wire has not been buried in the ground (and when larger than ½″ mesh is used). An occasional stripping of the top two or so inches of soil is necessary to sanitize this flooring.

Cement floors are ideal for cleaning, especially if drains have been built in to accommodate the overflow from hosing down the flight. Otherwise, any hard flooring that can be scrubbed easily is fine. Newspapers can be used to cover the floor. Wood shavings can be spread on top of these, allowing you to change the floor covering less often. Sand or peat moss can also be used, the latter being rather dusty if dry. Also, processed corn cob is available commercially. It's wise to clean small flights or cages with greater frequency, as the

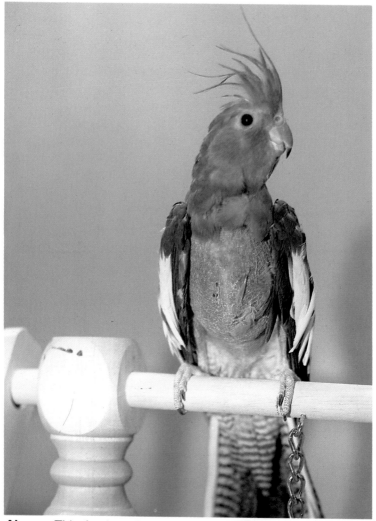

Above: This feather-plucked bird may be suffering from boredom or nutritional deficiencies. Photo by Tidbits Studio. **Facing page:** If young Cockatiels are allowed to become familiar with people, they will be very tame pets. Photo by Dr. Herbert R. Axelrod.

birds are more often in contact with the floor. Newspaper ink can stain the flight feathers of Lutinos, Pearl young and hens, and some Pieds (those with yellow or white tail feathers). For these birds, use paper toweling, wood shavings, sand, etc., especially if planning to show these birds.

In General

Plan ahead and plan wisely. A bird room or outside flight should be designed for efficiency. A sink should be close by for water and for scrubbing equipment. Cages and flights should be lined up so that food dishes are in front and can be checked at a glance, and refilled easily without running here and there. Keep in mind the possibility of future expansion in your plans. Cages and flights that are poorly constructed, hard to clean, and haphazardly situated can hamper efficiency and dampen all enthusiasm at chore time. Wise planning will allow you the time to sit back and enjoy your birds, instead of suffering with a poorly planned and impractical setup.

Equipment

Owning a single Cockatiel does not entail the array of equipment that is needed for a breeder with many birds. A pet bird's necessities are contained in his cage; i.e., water and seed containers, mineral block, perches, and maybe a toy or two. When housing many birds, the list lengthens considerably. Some of the following are not necessities but rather conveniences.

PERCHES. Have extra perches on hand (⅝" to ¾" dowels, or natural branches of comparable dimensions) to replace chewed, broken, or soiled ones. A wire brush is needed to scrub dirty perches, and a small knife to scrape off droppings. Natural branches need not be cleaned, but simply thrown out and replaced. Clean perches are important to the maintenance of healthy feet, beak, and facial areas. A bird uses his perch to rub extraneous food from his bill; provide him with a clean napkin.

WATER CONTAINERS. A seed cup, "pop bottle" font, or a plastic bottle may be used. The last I find most sanitary, as the water stays free of husks, food, or droppings. Various sizes may be purchased at any pet shop. The plastic bottles have metal tubes which contain a ball that withholds the water until the bird pushes it with his tongue or beak to release a drop. Cockatiels, being the curious characters they are, usually learn what this contraption is for very quickly. However, when first introduced, do not remove the previous familiar water container until you have seen the birds drink from the bottle. I prefer the green plastic to the clear, as algae does not form as quickly if kept in bright light, and vitamins or medicines will retain their potency longer. It is not sufficient to simply dump yesterday's water and refill with fresh. Scum builds up in any water container and must be washed out regularly. A bottle brush can be used for the bottle (a smaller bottle brush is needed for cleaning the metal tube). I have also found these plastic bottles and metal tubes dishwasher-safe on the top rack.

BATHING DISHES. Cockatiels, in general, are not avid bathers. However, they should be offered the opportunity, if not daily, at least once a week. Breeding birds must have a dish available at all times. Eggs need moisture to hatch easily, and parent birds seem to find bathing refreshing after a long sit in the nest box.

In my flights I use clay flower-pot saucers that are approximately 12″ in diameter and about 1½″ to 3″ deep. Each is placed atop an inverted flower pot, making a raised bird bath (floor litter and seeds are then less apt to get into the water). Spray-paint the outer surface, as clay is porous and the water will slowly ooze out. These unglazed clay containers are easier for the bird to grasp and walk on than a slippery finished surface is.

Above: Jelly Bean holding down the author's son, Jon. Photo by Nancy A. Reed. **Facing page:** A pet bird enjoying a treat. Photo by Horst Bielfeld.

FOOD CONTAINERS. These can be any size or shape, depending on the number of birds, amount or type of feed to be offered, etc. When many birds are to be fed, large gravity-type hoppers can be used. They must be checked periodically, as such containers can occasionally become clogged with husks. These are usually less wasteful (unless you have a "wise guy" that digs out all the seed, looking for his favorite kernels). The seed is also less apt to be contaminated by droppings.

When a breeder has a good number of birds, and thus feeders, it is thrifty to devise trays or place boxes directly under the seed holders to catch scattered uneaten kernels. These containers are periodically dumped into a holding bag or bin for recycling.

Single cups or dishes should not be deeper than 1″, as the bird can never get down that far once the empty husks build up on top. A larger, more shallow tray can be practical, especially for hard-working parent birds that should not be hampered in their feedings by having to waste time hunting around for uneaten seed.

It is wise to use the same sort of seed containers and water receptacles throughout. They will be easier and neater to store; more efficient to clean and fill in assembly-line fashion; and any bird that is switched from one cage or flight to another will immediately recognize his food source and not be temporarily deterred by the sight of a strange container.

If seed is bought in bulk, large jars containing the various seed mixes should be at hand to refill seed dishes. It is more efficient to refill these jars occasionally than to dig into a big storage barrel to refill each feeding receptacle.

NIGHT LIGHTS. It took a bird's broken neck to show me the necessity of this item, especially for birds in large flights. Cockatiels are prone to "night fright," and when one bird panics, so do the rest. (Be sure there is no possibility that rodents, cats, mites, etc., are the cause.) Several people have told me that their single pets have also exhibited this behavior in their cages at night. I've been asked if Cockies have bad dreams—who knows? But a tiny 7½-watt bulb can at least give enough light for the birds to tell what's where. It also enables parent birds to feed at night if they wish (especially in winter when nights are longer).

MITE SPRAYS. Mites are to birds as fleas are to dogs: at the least, very annoying. But more importantly, they can be disease carriers and, if allowed to go unchecked, are detrimental to the birds' health and sometimes fatal to young in the nest. Mites hide in dark crevices of perches and cage corners during the day, emerging at night to feed on the blood of the birds. Caged birds can be checked by covering the cage at night with a white cloth. In the early morning tiny red (blood-filled) mites will show up against the white. In a flight they can be detected by placing a white dish on the floor. The underside will expose them when turned over in the morning. If newspaper is used for floor covering, close examination of the side closest to the floor will show the telltale red dots. They are most prevalent in dry, hot weather.

Pet shops carry sprays or hanging disks which are sufficient for a single caged bird. For a large flock, one must locate an aviary and bird insecticide that comes in larger quantities. Always follow the directions exactly. Usually, all food, including gravel, salt spools, mineral blocks, cuttlebones, and water must be removed. Birds can remain in the flight, but do not purposely spray them directly, nor drench the place. A light misting three or four times a year is sufficient as a precaution against mites.

If a large infestation has developed (most prevalent in the summer), repeated spraying or foggings at seven-to-ten-day intervals two or three times is a must. Afterwards, if possible, drench the flight thoroughly with a strong spray of water from a hose; this can keep the mites in check. The floor litter in flights should be removed at least weekly in hot weather, as this is a good hiding place for mites during the day. Mites will infect all birds sooner or later, so precautions must be taken.

Above: Two hand-tame Cockatiels: a Pearl and a Pied. Photo by Isabelle Francais. **Facing page:** An adult Pearl male, indistinguishable from a Normal male except through records kept by the breeder. Photo by Horst Bielfeld.

NETS AND GLOVES. Netting is the easiest method of catching birds. Gloves are more often used to handle parrots, so that one's hands are not bitten. I dislike gloves for handling Cockatiels—you just can't feel what you're doing. A novice could squeeze a bird to death. I prefer to use a towel to cover and immobilize the bird, be it for claw clipping, medicating, or whatever.

CLAW CLIPPERS. There are specially designed claw clippers for birds; however, regular nail clippers or scissors will suffice.

FIRST AID. It is handy to have a basic first-aid kit of the following on hand: mercurochrome for cuts and marking fostered-out eggs or babies; Kwik-Stop to stop excessive bleeding; petroleum jelly to lubricate when banding or to soften a wound scab; Sal Hepatica and Pepto Bismol for digestive upsets; a heating pad to raise temperature for an ailing bird or unfeathered baby; and a hot-water bottle to transport eggs, young, or a sick bird. Pet shops carry an array of additional medicines and products.

HOSPITAL CAGE. Not a necessity but certainly a nicety if you have many birds. Although expensive, if it saves one or two birds, it has paid for itself. It is solid-walled (front: wire grid with a vertically sliding plastic panel), and it can be thermostatically controlled more evenly than when using a heating pad. Perches and seed cups are included. Additional saucers of water should be used to maintain adequate humidity in relation to the higher heat.

WINNOWING MACHINE. Like everything else these days, inflation has affected seed prices. Unfortunately, the U.S. economy is not the only factor to contend with. Bad weather can affect the law of supply-and-demand. Even international politics can raise havoc if we happen to have "strained relations" with countries that aviculturists depend on for imported seed. Our birds show little concern as they scatter seed helter skelter in search of their personal preferences—or walk through, play with, or dump receptacles at sheer whim. I find that the birds eat only 50% of the seed offered. This means half your seed money is wasted.

The principle of winnowing seed is very simple. Cockatiels husk each seed, ingesting only the kernel. The uneaten husks are much lighter in weight than a whole seed. By blowing the lighter-weight husks away, the heavier, uneaten seed can be reclaimed and refed. Pet owners do not need a machine. They can simply use their own lung power to blow the accumulated husks off their bird's seed cups. Even on gravity feeders, I either blow off or push off the accumulated husks twice a day, and push down fresh seed to refill the feed trough.

The most primitive way of winnowing seed is to just go out on a windy day and pour "used" seed from a stepladder, and let the wind blow the husks away, while a container directly below (a large basin or box) collects the good seed. A fan will also do a comparable job.

However, Dr. Richard Baer (President Emeritus of the American Federation of Aviculture and a charter member of A.C.S.) spent time inventing a winnowing machine. In his honor, we call it the "Baeromatic." In conjunction with the Baeromatic, a vacuum cleaner is needed to suck up the husks, and a container (I use a cardboard carton) to set the Baeromatic on top of to collect the good seed as it drops through the bottom of the machine. The beauty of the Baeromatic is that it can handle both large seeds (sunflower) at the same time as the smaller canary, millet, etc. If you wish to separate the salvaged sunflower from the smaller seeds for feeding separately, you can make a shallow box-type sieve using $1/8''$ wire mesh. The sunflower, hemp, and some oats will remain, while the smaller canary, millet, and some oats will sift through. (Petamine can also be winnowed to reclaim the uneaten thistle and canary seed, but of course the powdered portion will be sucked up by the vacuum cleaner).

Above: A Cockatiel allowed out of its cage, like this Pearl, often will be content to remain atop it. Photo by Horst Bielfeld.

Facing page: A Cinnamon Pearl Pied bird—the Cinnamon component is responsible for the light shade of gray. Photo by Horst Bielfeld.

Left: A Lutino in a cage with a door hinged at the bottom, making it easy for the bird to go in and out. Photo by Isabelle Francais.

The Baeromatic winnowing machine, showing a scoop of waste seed and winnowed seed in the container below. Photo by Nancy A. Reed.

A system must be devised to collect the seed scattered from the feeders. I do not suggest saving seed that accumulates on the floor of the cages or flights! Such seed will most certainly be contaminated by the birds' droppings, and possibly be moldy due to exposure to water (from spraying birds, or their bathing dishes). I have built recessed feeding stations on the exterior of my flights, with slide-out trays (muffin tins) set beneath and in front of the gravity feeders to collect the wasted seed. These are arranged so that it is almost impossible for the birds to contaminate the seed. (The collection trays are dumped daily into a container to save for future winnowing.) Be sure not to put seed feeders under overhead perches.

Directions for using the Baeromatic are simple. Place the machine on top of a collection container. Insert the nozzle of the vacuum cleaner through the hole in the back side of the Baeromatic. Turn the vacuum cleaner on, and slowly pour the seed into the trough-type opening in the front. The number of holes at the top of the machine should be covered according to seed being winnowed. If seed is not coming through clean (husks are still evident), cover more holes. When winnowing both sunflower and parakeet mix together, I usually run the seed through twice for more effectiveness. To winnow 50 lbs. of used seed will take about 30 minutes.

As I stated earlier, I find I can reclaim 50% of the original seed. However, once I am feeding recycled seed, I do not continue to save the waste. Oily seeds such as sunflower and hemp can eventually go rancid, although the smaller canary, millet, etc., have longer viability. If you winnow the same seed over and over, the seed will eventually become so stale as to be useless nutritionally. Winnow often when weather is warm.

WET/DRY VACUUM CLEANER. This is another luxury, but one I cannot now imagine doing without. A regular vacuum cleaner will pick up the thousand and three husks that accumulate, but the advantage of being able to vacuum water is a plus. Even without drains, you can do a thorough washing or hosing down of inside flights. It is even better if the machine has a spray attachment to use for mite sprays!

Left: A Pearl Cockatiel cracking a sunflower seed, the favorite food of many pet Cockatiels. Photo by Michael Gilroy.

Facing page: Delicate markings characterize the Cinnamon Pearl cross mutation. Photo by Horst Bielfeld.

Below: Two young Pearl Cockatiels, one a male, the other a female. Photo by Horst Bielfeld.

DIET

Diets in aviaries can be as varied as they are for humans around the world. There is no "official" diet, for birds or people. You can ask forty-two successful aviculturists for their bird's diet, and you will get forty-two different "recipes."

I base this chapter on my own experience, as well as including variations that others have found successful. A novice breeder may have to experiment until he finds a menu that seems to work most consistently for his birds. If your birds have been thriving and breeding consistently on shredded newspaper and Geritol (horrors!) then stick with it. Otherwise, add or subtract items one at a time.

I find that Cockatiels are not ones to accept new foods too quickly. Don't offer something one day and expect them to eat it immediately. If you feel strongly enough about some item, then you may have to persistently serve it as a side dish or mixed in with more familiar foods for weeks or even months before they accept it. A group of birds is easier to educate, in that if one bird so much as sniffs something new, the rest, being curious, will usually follow suit.

In recognizing a good basic diet for the Cockatiel, one must be familiar with the plains of Australia where the Cockatiel originated. In these western Australian plains there are high winds, months of dry, desertlike weather, and crops of small sun-dried seeds. These types of conditions should bring to mind the possibility of having birds that are not naturally familiar with many different types of foods. Conversely, consider the amazon parrot from the jungles of South America, where there is an abundance of fruits, nuts, and seeds to choose from. I think you get the picture: most amazons will readily accept new foods of varying tastes. All this discussion points to the fact that most Cockatiels are reluctant to accept new types of foods when first offered. Despite the fact that wild Cockatiels have not been imported for many decades, this inherent characteristic persists.

Again, birds are as individual as people. This individuality becomes especially noticeable when the birds are separated into breeding pairs. One couple may all but attack your hand as you put corn (or greens or conditioning foods, etc.) before them, while in the next cage you must remove yesterday's portion that was never or barely touched. I have had a cock that in his initial pairing devoured greens with gusto. Yet when mated with a different hen on the second nesting, he hardly noticed his salad course again! I've decided the only difference between some people I know and the various birds I have is that the latter wear feathers. They are all equally confusing to me at times!

If your Cockatiel has just been purchased, be sure you inquire about the diet the bird has been receiving, so that you can at least duplicate that diet initially, even if that diet is not what you feel is best. Your new Cockatiel is already stressed from adjusting to a new environment, and a change in its diet at this time would be even more stressful. Feeding the bird the diet it is accustomed to will allow it to get sufficient food. If it came from a pet shop, it will probably have only been fed on a maintenance level. Little by little you can change the diet to fulfill the nutritional requirements you feel are essential to your particular bird.

Water

Water is a subject that is seldom given more notice than a couple of sentences. Yet any living creature will die more quickly due to lack of water than through lack of food.

We humans take water for granted. How many people actually drink a glass or two of pure water a day? Our daily

A pair of Lutino Cockatiels. Photo by Bill Parlee.

fluid needs are satisfied by coffee, tea, milk, soda, etc. Aside from the amount of moisture ingested from greens, corn, or fruit, a bird must depend entirely on whatever water supply is available, however dirty the offering.

Various watering devices have been designed: pop and plastic bottles are the most commonly used. Unlike open cups or dishes, the water supply in these bottles is not easily contaminated by droppings or food. However, with these, the temptation is greater not to change and clean them is greater. I make it a daily rule and ritual to change and clean them no matter how little water has been consumed. But still, an unchanged water bottle is better than a dish of two-day-old, dirty water.

Daily water changes become even more necessary in warm weather, or when vitamins were added to the water the previous day. Algae and bacteria will build up more rapidly under such conditions.

It is so easy to neglect this area of a bird's diet. Water is cheap, accessible, and seemingly unimportant as far as nutrition is concerned. When I start to feel lazy about changing and cleaning water bottles, I ask myself: Would *I* drink the water from that receptacle? If I hesitate at the thought, that is enough incentive to be thorough.

Water is the most underestimated part of the diet. Yet, again, it is more vital than food itself. Consistently clean water and containers are as worthy of attention as is your bird's food.

Protein—Carbohydrate—Fat

Let's get to the fundamentals of nutrition. We must give our birds a menu that includes an adequately balanced ratio of protein, carbohydrate, and fat. Aside from vitamins and minerals, these three are the major nutritional components of all foods. When the proper combination of these elements is present in the diet, there is a much better chance of producing a show bird, a good breeder, or a happy pet.

Most recently, pelleted food has gained favor with many aviculturists—it may be *the* bird diet of the future. This is a "state of the art" method of ensuring a nutritionally balanced diet. Compacted into pellets or crumbles of different sizes, appropriate formulas are made up for different species of birds. The *extruded* pellets are the preferred form. Such a diet does sound very practical and efficient, as it eliminates much waste and the mess from seed hulls. My only concern would be selling or buying birds that didn't know what a seed was. Using pellets as a supplement to a seed diet is an alternative.

With seed as the major food source for Cockatiels, there is seldom, if ever, a danger of insufficient carbohydrates or fats. Grains in general are all high in carbohydrates, while certain seeds contain more fat (oil) than others.

Carbohydrates are the sugars and starches in seeds. Carbohydrates and fats are much alike: both produce heat and energy. Fats, however, are sources of some essential fatty acids which aid in the absorption of some vitamins and minerals.

When a bird is obese we call him fat. Actually, this is good terminology, as excess foods are generally stored in the body as fats. A Cockatiel that gets fat is probably eating too many fatty foods and not getting enough exercise to burn it off. A fat bird, regardless of age, is a candidate for many health-related problems.

Birds (especially inactive ones) require only a minimal amount of fat in their diet. However, those seeds with a higher oil content (sunflower, safflower, oats, hemp, flax, niger) are valuable during the colder months, as they are heat producers. Remember though, when stocking up on seed, that oily seeds cannot be stored for long periods of time without going rancid. Canary and millet seed (low in oils) can be held under optimum conditions (ventilated, cool, and dry) for a year or more. Sunflower, hemp, etc., should be purchased in smaller amounts and more frequently, most especially during the summer months or if you live in a warm, humid climate.

Protein is the component that is most apt to be lacking in a Cockatiel's diet. Signs of deficiency are poor plumage on adult birds and slow growth of young in the nest. While carbohydrates and fat are basically needed as fuel for energy (physical performance), protein is necessary for physical growth: the bird's feathers, muscles, organs, and all that makes him a physical being.

Proteins are composed of amino acids. Some of the amino acids cannot be manufactured by your bird and must be supplemented in the diet. You may have heard the phrase "essential amino acids." This refers to the basic need of your bird to have proteins in sufficient quantities to be used by the body when needed: for muscle growth, regeneration of body tissue, and the like.

Obviously, sufficient protein is most important when young are growing in the nest. A breeder can tell easily in the first fourteen days which chick is two days older then the next younger sibling. In human infants this would be comparable to at least a two-month difference in age. The growth rate is truly phenomenal. Adequate protein in the diet is extremely important at this time. Be aware of foods that can supply more protein.

Among seeds, canary is high in protein content. Thistle (niger) is even higher; however, it is often not as easy to purchase nor is it always accepted by Cockies in their staple diet. Some breeders will accustom their birds to egg-food recipes that canary breeders use. Petamine and similar conditioning mixes contain powdered egg and milk which are suitable. I use gelatin in the mix that I sprinkle on corn. Brewer's yeast is another source of protein. Many people recommend grinding up Purina Monkey Chow, and adding it to the seed, the Petamine, or the conditioning or nestling food; or it may be fed whole, separately, if the birds will accept it (attach a piece to the cage wires with a clip). I have recently heard of a powdered cottage cheese. Some greens also offer higher protein content than others: comfrey especially, and collards are good.

I am sure there are other sources that I have yet to hear of, but if one realizes the best source of protein is through some form of animal products (egg, gelatin, etc.), one can improvise. The difficulty is incorporating these usually powdered ingredients into a diet that consists mainly of seed. But if you are consistent and persistent in keeping such mixtures before the birds, you will find they will accept them—in fact, devour them when the need is greatest: while breeding and during the molt. Offer ample portions when they need and will consume the most, but certainly offer them year round in minimal amounts. The birds will therefore remain familiar with them and still keep to a diet balanced for the less stressful periods.

Seed Quality
First and above all, buy the best-quality seed available. Grains should contain a minimum of dust and never smell sour or rancid. (Taste-test for sweetness yourself!) It drives me up a wall when bargain hunters buy their seed according to the price tag, brag about their minimal cost, and then complain that their birds breed poorly and are never in good enough condition to exhibit at show time. Most cheap seed is very likely old seed. It has lost much or most of its nutritional value. No bird can reach tiptop condition on it, and if babies are produced, most likely they will be of poor quality. A bird is only as good as what it eats. If you must constantly cut corners to feed and care for forty birds, then limit yourself to twenty birds. Feed and care for these in royal fashion, and your production will most likely be equal to whatever your forty birds could have produced, with far better quality.

Most importantly, get to know your dealer and let him know all of your seed needs. Usually a dealer will be glad to order what you need if it is not on hand. Should you live in a more remote area, you may find that you will have to get your seeds from a national seed house by mail or United Parcel Service. Many of these seed houses are mentioned or advertised in national cage-bird magazines.

Whenever you buy or order large amounts of seed, be sure that you have a cool, dry place to store them. Seeds stored in warm places tend to get webby, and seeds will get moldy if there is dampness. Small amounts of seed may be stored in the refrigerator. This will keep them fresh. Conditioning mixes should always be refrigerated in the summer. Never freeze seeds, as this will kill the seed, and upon thawing the seed will dry out and lose its nutritional value. "Webby," or "buggy" seed is not a problem for your birds (actually, the bugs and larvae provide more protein); however, it can be a source of irritation when seed moths start invading the living areas of your home.

How to Feed

Some aviculturists choose to serve different seeds in separate dishes, so that the birds won't whisk out the less relished seeds in search of their favorites. Such a setup can prove less wasteful. The parakeet mix should be served separately from the sunflower seed. Petamine or conditioning foods are always best served in small containers.

An alternate procedure is to combine all the basic seeds in a properly balanced ratio and offer the mixture in one feeder. (A suggested mix is 40% millet, 30% sunflower, 15% canary seed, 5% hulled oats, 5% safflower, and 5% hemp). The reasoning behind this practice is that Cockatiels will be less likely to eat too much "candy" and not enough "liver."

Over the years I have seen birds that will eat only sunflower seeds. The birds were obese and their feathers a mess. Upon advising their owners to feed smaller amounts of sunflower mixed with larger amounts of millet and canary seed, the birds were forced to eat more of the other seeds than they had previously. After a few short months many of these birds had been cured of a very bad habit. However, most birds will eat a balanced diet of their own choice, varying it according to their immediate needs.

Cockatiels husk each seed, removing the shell casing and eating only the kernel itself. These husks are often dropped back into the seed dish, and a novice bird owner has often mistaken a dish full of husks for a full and uneaten dish of seed. Many birds have died of starvation because their well-meaning but unknowing owners were unaware of their pet's feeding habits. These husks must be blown off frequently to expose the whole and uneaten seed beneath. A dish three inches deep will not supply a bird with feed longer than a dish one inch deep. Husks build up on top, and the two inches of good seed below is covered by the empty husks above.

You will find that, at different times of the year, some seeds are eaten more than others: most especially and rightfully sunflower seed while young are being fed. Sunflower husks, being large, can cover smaller, uneaten seeds. Therefore it is sometimes imperative that the major offering of sunflower be given in a separate dish. At breeding and weaning times, during cold weather, or when otherwise trying to "beef up" birds, extra oats and hemp might also be offered in small, supplemental portions.

Basic Seeds

It is a variety of seeds that makes up 90% of a Cockatiel's diet. Therefore, to belabor a point, the quality of the seed is very important. Poor seed provides poor nutrition. While seed-mix recipes can vary with individual breeders or regions of the country, the most usual staple diet consists of parakeet mix (canary, millet, and oats), sunflower seed, and Petamine or a conditioning food.

Let us discuss these staple seeds and mixtures individually.

PARAKEET MIX. This is made up of varying ratios (depending on the particular seed company's recipe or the breeder who mixes his own) of canary, millet and oat seeds. There is also a mix put out by various commercial seed companies called Cockatiel mix. This combines the above three seeds, plus sunflower, hemp, and possibly other variety seeds. Some also include safflower.

CANARY SEED. This we have previously mentioned as higher in the percentage of protein than most seeds. Moroccan canary seed is considered superior in quality to domestic canary. This particular seed is one of the easiest seeds that newly fledged birds can husk, and should be offered in extra portions at weaning time.

MILLET. This grain comes in many varieties, but the large white proso millet is used in parakeet mix. It is valuable less for its nutrients than as a source of fiber and bulk in the diet. Millet helps slow down the digestive process in order that the nutrients from the more valuable seeds are absorbed without passing through too quickly.

OATS. This seed is considered high in fat and carbohydrates and is valuable as a "heat producer." It can be fattening for inactive birds or those in warmer climates. It is also one of the easiest seeds for fledgling birds to eat.

SUNFLOWER. This particular seed is offered for sale under different classifications as to size or color—giant gray through black. Many people assume that the larger the seed, the higher the quality—not so! The smaller, cheaper, black sunflower is actually higher in oil content than the grays. But depending on your climate and the activity of your bird, the small, black sunflower may be too fattening.

Sunflower seed is offered as the main ingredient of a parrot mix, which also includes raw peanuts (husked and unhusked), dried corn kernels (usually left untouched by Cockatiels), some oats and hemp, and dried red peppers. If you also own larger psittacines, you might offer a mixture of both the parrot mix and giant gray (or whatever grade) sunflower to all your hookbills in a ratio of two parts straight sunflower to one part parrot mix. Cockatiels will learn to nibble on the raw husked peanuts (high in protein and nutrients) as well as most of the other ingredients.

As mentioned, sunflower is a fattening seed, being high in oil content. It is most particularly relished and needed by parents feeding young in the nest. Remember that any seed that is high in oils does not store well for long periods of time.

Variety Seeds

I have mentioned that niger (thistle) is high in oil and protein. It has become a rarer and therefore expensive seed, and Cockatiels fortunately do not depend on it. It is included in Petamine and conditioning mixes. Again, it does not store well, being high in oil content.

Hemp seed is another now expensive seed, but is much more readily accepted than niger. It also is high in fat and does not store well. It can cause inactive birds to become obese. If you purchase a Cockatiel mix which contains hemp, this should be sufficient. However, an extra portion prior to the breeding season is valuable in inducing birds to reach top breeding condition.

Safflower seed has been proposed as perhaps a less fattening and a better alternative to sunflower seed. It is said to produce a glossier plumage. However, studies have proven that safflower should be a supplement and not a total replacement for sunflower.

Millet sprays are a favorite of Cockatiels. These are higher in protein than the regular millets, and should be offered daily, especially to parents feeding young. This is another kind of seed that is easy for fledglings to husk, and therefore should be readily available at weaning time. I suggest that one purchase millet sprays at the cheaper bulk rate, as they will keep well over a long period of time.

Using the seeds from my purchased millet, for several years I have grown a small crop of spray millet in our summer vegetable garden with good results. A friend had phenomenal success by providing a rich mulch of compost and manures to the soil. His heads averaged two feet in length and three inches in width. However, one year his crop was demolished by a severe thunderstorm just as the sprays were reaching full growth. The heads were so heavy that the stems broke in the high winds and downpour. Heavy twine or rope-support fences are recommended between the rows to minimize such losses.

It is more practical for the owner of one or two Cockatiels to purchase millet sprays in dozen packs or five-pound boxes from a reputable pet dealer. Check the sprays before you purchase them. If the stems are pliable, the millet is fresh.

Conditioning Supplements
Under this category, Petamine (put out by the Kellogg Seed Company of Milwaukee, Wisconsin) is the most widely recognized mix. Petamine contains niger, lettuce, rape, and canary seeds, dried skimmed milk, ground corn, sesame, flax, poppy, teazle, oat groats, brewer's yeast, anise, tricalcium phosphate, dicalcium phosphate, calcium carbonate, sodium chloride, wheat-germ meal, and cod-liver oil. Guaranteed analysis: crude protein, min. 22%; crude fat, min. 15%; crude fiber, max. 7%; ash, max. 7%.

Other seed companies offer their own condition and nestling mixes consisting of similar ingredients. The purpose of such supplements is to ensure a balanced diet. Caged birds cannot thrive or reproduce on just seed alone. These mixes will provide the protein that is most apt to be deficient in seed, as well as extra vitamins, minerals, and other nutrients.

Such powdered mixes should be stored in a tight container in a cool, dry place. During hot, humid weather, order only on a month-to-month basis to ensure top nutritional value.

Chick starter has also been used extensively and is recommended highly by many aviculturists. This can be bought at any feed store that carries poultry supplies. It is reasonable in price and is nutritious.

A supplement used by many older aviculturists is "milk sop." This consists basically of whole-wheat bread (or any other highly nutritious bread) dampened with milk. If you cannot be around to remove the leftovers before it sours, then water is a better bet for moisture. Some people add honey and vitamins to the milk or water, or sprinkle a powdered vitamin on the moistened bread.

More recent discussion suggests that birds cannot properly break down, digest, and utilize dairy nutrients. I'm not a scientist, nor have I personally fed milk sop, but it has been used by aviculturists for so many decades previously that I feel it worth mentioning.

Other supplements that can be offered, though not necessarily needed if any of the above are supplied, are monkey chow, wheat germ (especially valuable at breeding time), and corn meal.

Greens and Fruit

Greens are a necessary and natural source of vitamins and nutrients. Depending on the season or climate, it is of course ideal to be able to pick greens fresh. During winter months one may have to rely on market produce. But no matter where you get the greens, wash them thoroughly. Even if picked from your own unsprayed garden, do not discount the possibility of a neighbor's dog mistaking your greenery for a fire hydrant, or of a passing wild bird's indiscretion. There have been fatal incidents where chemical sprays have carried over from another garden in the neighborhood.

There is enough variety, even at the market, not to resort to varieties of head lettuce, which are 92% water and low in nutrients. The greener the leaf, the better. Consider collards, kale, swiss chard, spinach, romaine lettuce, watercress, etc., as well as the tops of radishes, carrots, and turnips. And depending on your geographic location, there are probably more alternatives. While old wives' tales persist that mustard greens and parsley are toxic, these have proven false.

Many wild weeds in season are suitable, nutritious, and free (but wash them well!). Dandelion and chickweed, most homeowner's enemies, can become a valuable food source for your birds.

While my Cockatiels will not readily accept constant changes in their salad course, chickweed seems to be the one and only green that does not need to be impressed on them. In the early spring, when it is most prevalent and succulent here, I venture forth with an army's provision of containers to dig chickweed from foreign fields (which I have located over a few years of reconnaissance). In view of the effort, it is somewhat disheartening to have the harvest literally devoured within less time than it took to obtain!

Aside from the seasonal chickweed, I feed collard greens year 'round, as my market stocks them consistently. Collards are high in vitamins A and C, minerals, and contain a protein content comparable to corn. The greatest concentrations of nutrients is in the stem and veins of the leaf, which the birds seem naturally to prefer.

I also grow collards in my garden, setting out young plants in early spring (they will withstand some frost), and I have been able to pick leaves well into January here in New England! Warmer climates should be able to offer a continual crop, as south of Virginia it is considered a biennial.

If obtaining greens is a problem for you, at the very least use packaged dry greens, available at your local pet shop. They are surprisingly good and will supplement your seed diet.

Various fruits and vegetables are also suitable; most commonly apples, corn, and carrots. The last is more readily eaten if grated. Let's face it, any fruit or vegetable that your Cockatiels will eat is beneficial to them.

Some people offer such produce daily, twice a day, or only several times a week. But whatever the frequency, always promptly remove any wilted greens, or browned fruit or vegetables, before they become moldy and therefore possible sources of digestive problems.

Minerals

While minerals are available from seeds, greens, vitamins, and water, it is a simple matter to ensure a more adequate supply by offering a mineral block and cuttlebone, plus a gravel-grit mix.

Mineral deficiencies will become most evident at breeding time. Extra calcium and phosphorus are vital for the hen to produce eggs and for the tremendous skeletal growth in nestlings. I offer both cuttlebone and a mineral block, as some birds will show a preference for one over the other. The mineral block, being harder, is also good for exercising the beak and keeping it trim.

While mineral blocks can be bought at your local pet center, you can also make your own "cubes" at home. The following recipe has been widely used: 4–5 parts plaster of paris; 3 parts powdered calcium carbonate; 4 parts bone meal. Add enough water to mix. Pour into small containers (a muffin pan is good), and insert U-shaped wires into the mix. Allow several days to harden. Attach to the cage by the exposed wire ends.

In addition I offer a gravel-grit mix in a small container. I use parakeet gravel (#2) mixed 50:50 with Red Cross Grit (which is pink in color because of the iodine content).

The use of gravel and grit has become a controversial subject lately. Some breeders believe it may be one cause of their birds "going light." Theoretically, birds that husk each seed should not need an abrasive to help digest the kernels. My large parrots that I have now had over fifteen years do not have any gravel mixture offered them, for the simple reason that all they do is dump the mix and mutilate the container. Yet they remain in top condition.

However, I do continue to feed my Cockatiels the gravel mix. (Some breeders substitute oyster shell for grit). To date, I have never experienced problems with birds "going light," and the Cockies relish their daily offerings of the mineral supplement. Having talked with many people, I believe the gravel problem may mostly involve Budgerigars. However, many Cockatiel breeders have discontinued feeding gravel with no adverse effects. I personally choose to continue the supplement, both because my birds enjoy it and have had no

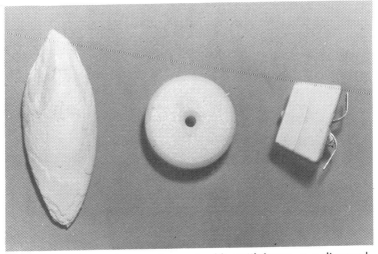

Mineral requirements may be met with cuttlebone, a salt spool, and a mineral block. Photo by Nancy A. Reed.

problems and because I am too Scotch to throw out the two-year supply that I have on hand. After that, I shall probably discontinue its use.

I once mixed a commercial bird charcoal with my gravel mix, and the birds loved it. But I have since been advised that charcoal can absorb vitamins A and K, so I have stopped its general use. However, it is a natural sweetener and can prove beneficial to a bird with a sour crop. After such a problem is corrected, discontinue its use.

Commercial mineral supplementation in aviculture is a relatively new procedure. In years past we provided cuttlebone, oyster shell (calcium), etc., and thought that was all that was necessary. Lately, however, mineral supplementation, either liquid or powder, has proven in controlled studies to resolve many deficiencies in our birds' diet and has lessened the incidence of disease.

An item to consider in this discussion on minerals is *salt*. During breeding season, some source of salt seems to become more of a necessity than a nicety. I have found very little to read on the subject and thus must go mainly on experience.

Birds, like people and animals, enjoy and apparently *need* some salt. A bird's demand for salt is greatest during the breeding season.

For each breeding pair, I supply a rabbit salt spool. Mine are white, but I understand that there is a pink variety which offers more iodine. I attach these to the wires of the breeding pens. In fact, I find it saves the parent birds some effort if the spools are attached close to the water source, as it takes moisture on the tongue to lick any appreciable amount from the spool. I also include salt in the mix that I sprinkle on the fresh corn. Those people who cannot purchase salt spools locally might consider offering iodized table salt in a small container. But be *stingy,* so that your birds do not overindulge, as granular salt is too easily ingested.

Lugol's solution (an iodine solution that can be purchased at the drug store with a doctor's prescription) was suggested to me years back, and I have offered it once a month: 1 teaspoon per gallon of water. Perhaps it is not necessary, what with the salt spools and Red Cross grit, but I have continued to use it. Until problems arise, why change? Iodine, I have read, is important in regard to fertility.

Vitamins

We all know that vitamins and minerals are important to proper nutrition in all animals. With birds these essential nutrients take on added importance, as our birds are limited to what we offer them in their daily diet. In the wild, birds would forage for their fare naturally and satisfy these nutritional requirements from the choice of nutrients available to them, especially minerals. We can't always be sure we are providing all the necessary elements of a healthy diet, so the solution entails supplementation with vitamins and minerals.

Theoretically, with a varied daily diet of fresh seeds, greens, etc., vitamin supplementation is more an assurance to the owner's peace of mind than a genuine need of the birds. However, in this health-kick day and age, there is no harm or waste in offering vitamins once or twice a week in water, or sprinkling powdered forms lightly on some food source daily or a few times a week. In times of stress, vitamins can prove more of a necessity. But don't shoot for overkill when the birds are generally fine.

Some of the symptoms of vitamin and mineral deficiencies are: generally weak or lethargic birds, poor feather quality, nails and beaks that grow abnormally or that become overgrown too quickly, small clutches of eggs, or poor hatchability of eggs, soft-shelled eggs, respiratory problems, eye infections, infertility—and the list goes on and on. Often some owners will treat their Cockatiel for an illness when the bird is suffering from a dietary deficiency. Deficiencies in the diet can mimic the symptoms of many ailments.

In the past, and even currently, many bird breeders use cod-liver oil for its vitamin A and D, and wheat-germ oil for Vitamin E (most necessary at breeding time). These oils can be mixed with the seed in the ratio of one tablespoon to one pound of seed. Do not mix a greater quantity than can be consumed in a day or two, as oils can become rancid.

More recently, birds have finally become big-enough business to warrant more extensive research into their specific nutritional needs. This has resulted in both powdered and liquid vitamins formulated especially for avian requirements. There are now even vitaminized seeds and vitaminized pelleted foods for birds.

In the past, many people used baby vitamins. These human vitamin supplements were made to be added to liquids and consumed immediately. When offered to birds in their water, the vitamins will lose potency as quickly as within a half hour. Use bird vitamins. These are purposely designed to retain potency in water for longer periods of time. There are now many brands on the market, and if they are specifically formulated for birds, they can be recommended. However, in my opinion, the dosage recommended on some labels is too strong, which makes the water distasteful to the birds. Cockatiels can readily avoid drinking vitaminized water for twenty-four hours. Thus your good intentions and money literally go down the drain. I add just enough to tint the water pale yellow.

Many breeders use liquid and powdered vitamins both. Liquid vitamins are less wasteful if the breeder can calculate the amount of water the birds usually consume in twenty-four hours. Powdered vitamins can blow or fall off the food they're mixed with, or the coating of vitamins may not be totally consumed as husks are discarded.

Previously, breeders resorted to dog vitamins. This is not bad, but such supplements contain Vitamin D_2, whereas birds require Vitamin D_3. Check your labels.

The vitamin that is likely to be most lacking in a diet basically consisting of seed is Vitamin B_{12}, which is especially needed during the breeding season. This vitamin is most commonly available naturally in animal by-products, such as dairy foods (eggs, gelatin, cheese etc.). Petamine and other conditioning mixes contain dried milk and egg, or both. A full-spectrum vitamin will ensure an additional source. Be sure the vitamins you are feeding include the B vitamins.

Finally, the perches your birds stand upon can be a bonus source of nutrients as they whittle them down during leisure time. I understand that willow contains an ingredient used in aspirin. Sassafras and apple branches are said to be beneficial and are also relished by the birds. Most probably, whatever *fresh* branches you can provide will be a natural source of nutrients.

In summary, your birds are only as good as what they eat. Seed and water alone will not produce or maintain any bird in top condition. Expand your menu. The more variety, the more balanced the diet will be, and the less the likelihood of protein, vitamin, and mineral deficiencies.

(My appreciation to Bill Parlee for contributing his knowledge, experience, and writing to this chapter.)

COMMON AILMENTS AND DISEASES

by Richard E. Baer, D.V.M.,
and Al Decoteau, D.V.M.

Methods of Cure

The method of treatment for most sick Cockatiels should begin with the provision of warmth and high humidity. Because of a bird's very high metabolic rate (average body temperature 104°F), provision of warmth (heat) helps immediately in giving the sick bird a chance to recover.

Warmth can be provided in the simplest way by a light bulb close to the cage or by a heating pad above or beneath the cage in which the sick bird is confined. The temperature should be kept at between 85° and 90°F. But regulation of humidity is difficult in these arrangements. Do not use the commercial vaporizers available from most drug stores, as they will emit spits of scalding water along with the steam.

The cage should be covered on all sides except the front with a large towel to conserve heat. The front is left uncovered so that light may enter; this is important so that the sick bird can see to eat and drink.

By far the most satisfactory method of providing warmth and humidity is by using a hospital cage, either a commercially manufactured one or one of your own making. Commercial cages need some minor modifications to adapt them for use with Cockatiels. Often the perch is too high and the cage is too small to allow the bird to fly up to it, nor any way for the bird to climb up. Also, most commercial hospital cages have no means for providing proper relative humidity. With the optimal dry-bulb temperature of 85–90°F, the relative humidity within the hospital cage should be maintained between 70% and 80%. This can be accomplished by placing

A commercially available hospital cage of conventional design. Photo by Nancy A. Reed.

several small containers of water inside the cage.

Relative humidity can be measured with a hygrometer or the correct relative humidity can be approximated by using the following rule of thumb: The surface area of the water should be approximately 2% of the total volume of the cage. (Example: A cage 12″ x 10″ x 10″ = 1200 cu. in. Two percent of 1200 = 24; therefore, 24 sq. in. of water surface is needed.)

The sick bird will drink more liquid in the high-temperature environment of the hospital cage, and if water-soluble medicines are used, the bird will be consuming more medicine. If water-soluble medicines are administered, all of the water receptacles used to provide humidity should be filled with the medicated water. Because of high evaporation at the

85-90° temperature, there should be ample medicated water in the cage at all times; it should be changed at least once, or preferably twice, daily.

A hospital cage of your own design must make provision for regulating heat and humidity. Safe and reliable ceramic heating units with thermostats are available from avicultural supply houses. Anyone with several Cockatiels will find the hospital cage to be a necessary piece of equipment. (It can also serve as a brooder for hand-raised chicks, or even as an isolation cage for the observation of new birds.)

Except in the cases of ailments or diseases having pathognomonic symptoms, the bird owner will not usually be able to make a definite diagnosis when he observes that his Cockatiel is sick. He may be able to come to some nonspecific conclusion; for example: that the bird has a respiratory ailment or that it has some form of enteritis.

In all of these situations, treatment will be more or less general: confinement to the hospital cage with increased warmth and humidity and the administration of a water-soluble antibiotic, such as the Terramycin powders. Ornacyn, Neo-Terramycin, and Egg-Terramycin (¼ tsp. per qt. of water) are readily available from various sources and should be kept on hand always. Timely action will often prevent a catastrophe.

After apparent recovery, the bird should be left in the hospital cage for at least two days and observed closely. After this, a few additional days of confinement will be needed while the hospital-cage temperature is brought down to normal (about 8°F every 12 hrs). Do not be in too big a hurry to return the bird to its regular cage or flight.

After its return, continue to observe it closely; and if there is any indication of a possible relapse, return it to the hospital cage for additional confinement and treatment.

Respiratory Infections

These may vary from a slight "cold," with sneezing and a nasal discharge ("runny nose") or plugged-up nostrils, to pneumonia with severe respiratory difficulty. It may be the result of lowered resistance and stamina brought on by over-sheltering; due to exposure to drafts or sudden temperature changes and chilling; secondary to generalized infectious disease; or it may be attributable to a combination of these causes.

Treatment is as described above: confinement with heat and high humidity, together with the administration of a water-soluble antibiotic. In respiratory infections the high humidity tends to break up the congestion which causes the sick bird stress and anxiety. With congestion relieved, the bird will be more responsive to treatment.

This author prefers to handle sick birds as little as possible and to utilize direct medication only when absolutely necessary. Restraining a sick bird often causes overstressing and may do more harm than the proposed medication does good, as the sick bird could die of shock from the handling. If the sick bird does not appear to be overly stressed, is tame and can be easily restrained, in the case of simple rhinitis ("cold"), one may want to unplug the nostrils with a cotton swab and apply a little Vicks Vapor-Rub around them. A few drops of oil of eucalyptus in the drinking water, as an expectorant, may be beneficial in the cases of chronic colds and coughs.

There is one form of chronic respiratory infection for which there is no completely adequate treatment. This is a form of mold infection known as aspergillosis. Its symptoms may vary from minimal respiratory distress often brought on by exercise, to nothing more than reduced appetite and a gradual weight loss ("going light"). Cockatiels may make a "cheeping" sound when breathing. The condition is more apt to be seen in a bird that has been imported, or kept under crowded conditions, and exposed to mold spores.

Prevention is the best safeguard against this infection. Feed only seed that is clean and not moldy, and clean the cage or flight frequently so that seed hulls, spilled seed, fruit, or greens mixed with droppings do not have a chance to become wet and nurture the growth of mold on the cage or aviary floor.

Enteritis

Inflammation of the intestines is primarily manifested by diarrhea (abnormal droppings, which may vary from green-and-watery to bloody). The diarrhea may cause soiling of the feathers around the vent and may or may not be accompanied by systemic changes in the bird, such as fluffing up, malaise, husking seeds but refusing to eat them, and perching on both feet. Without a doubt, this is the most common disease condition noted in pet birds. It may be a primary condition or it may be secondary to a generalized disease.

As a primary condition, it can be brought on by chilling, excessive drafts, rapid temperature fall, change in diet, contaminated feed, or even sudden fright. Simple noninfectious diarrhea (watery droppings) may be the result of feeding too much fruit or greens and can be alleviated simply by removing the cause.

It is safest, however, to assume that all enteritises are infectious, especially if some systemic changes are noted, and to initiate immediately the standard hospital-cage treatment with antibiotics.

Prevention involves eliminating the causes: chillings, drafts, excessive temperature changes, sudden changes in diet, etc., together with care in purchasing and feeding of clean feed. Make sure your purveyor of seed does not store it in open bins where it could be contaminated by droppings from rats or other vermin, and store your own feed in vermin-proof containers.

Egg Binding

Egg binding is an ailment of the laying Cockatiel hen that cannot be considered uncommon. It may be the result of cold, but it is more apt to be seen in the over-producing hen or the hen whose diet may be deficient in calcium. It has been suggested that a drop in the level of blood calcium might be the underlying factor causing a state of spasm or cramp in the oviduct, resulting in a stasis of the egg. Such an egg is seemingly normal in all appearances, but may be thin-shelled in some cases.

The affected Cockatiel is often found on the floor of the cage, completely listless, but as a rule, bright of eye and alert. Palpation will generally reveal the egg stalled inside the vent.

The heated hospital cage, with the relative humidity as close to saturation as possible, is the ideal treatment to relieve this spasm or cramping of the oviduct. Then the egg should pass within 24 hours. As the hen is not organically sick, no medication is needed. I do not personally favor such treatments as steaming, lubrication, or manipulation.

Occasional cases of extreme difficulty in egg laying can result in a temporary paralysis, which will persist as long as two weeks or more. Good nursing care is required in these rare instances, with the sick bird remaining in the hospital cage.

The incidence of egg binding can be greatly lessened with improvements in feeding and management; providing a complete diet supplemented with minerals, multi-vitamins, and adequate exercise. One should refrain from overbreeding, and the hen that persists in laying eggs without sitting should be discouraged from laying for a while by removing the nest box. Hens that become egg bound should be rested for at least 60 days after recovery.

Crop Binding
This condition, also known as crop impaction, is seen more often in young Cockatiels than in adults, and can be a problem in hand-fed young. Its cause is usually attributed to overfeeding by the parents or the hand-feeder. Occasionally, a bird that has been denied grit for some time will gorge on it when again available and develop an impacted crop.

To restrain the bird without injury, it is best to wrap it in a towel, catching it as quickly and with as little commotion as possible. A few drops of mineral oil, followed by gentle manipulation, should ease the crop binding. In more stubborn cases, it may be necessary to manipulate the crop mass with the head down, emptying the crop of its contents by massaging it in the direction of the mouth. An eyedropper or two full of warm water, given before starting the massage, may help. After the crop is emptied, a few drops of mineral oil may be given.

Recurrence may be prevented by limiting grit, offering more soft food, especially greens, and perhaps prompting increased water consumption by providing a salt block. New birds should be introduced gradually to grit by mixing a small quantity at first with the seed.

Crop Sickness

Also called "sour crop," this may be caused by bad food or be secondary to acute indigestion or catarrhal cold. A Cockie with sour crop vomits a watery fluid from the beak continuously. This should not be confused with normal regurgitation between breeding Cockatiels. Treatment calls for the administration of Kaopectate (1 drop every 3 hours) or bicarbonate of soda (mix ½ teaspoon to a cup of water, then administer an eyedropperful every 3 hours). Calcium propionate, the preservative used in poultry feed, is available from poultry supply houses. It can be tried both as a treatment and as a preventative (use ¼ teaspoon to 2 qts. of water). Success in using this product to prevent sprouted seed from souring has also been reported.

Conjunctivitis

This condition appears as a watery discharge from the eye. The eyelids may become swollen to the extent that a temporary blindness occurs. It may be the result of primary infection or secondary to respiratory infections.

Treatment consists in the application of an antibiotic ophthalmic ointment available at the drug store (not one containing Streptomycin, which is dangerous to birds).

Overgrown Beak and Claws

In the older Cockatiel the upper mandible sometimes grows too long, often becoming distorted. Trimming is best accomplished by restraining the bird, wrapped in a towel, and using a claw clipper in conjunction with a sharp pair of scissors.

Cockatiels are not usually affected by overgrown claws. If the condition does occur, hold the claw in good light to locate the blood vessel, then cut off the tip with claw clippers, beyond the blood vessel. If bleeding should occur, dip the claw in flour, hydrogen peroxide (household strength), or in iron-sulfate powder (Monsel's salts). The last, sold in most pet shops under brand names such as Kwik Stop, should always be on the bird-medicine shelf. A lit cigarette, held to the end of the claw, will serve as an emergency cautery in the case of persistent bleeding.

Sore Foot

Also known as bumble foot, it can occur in Cockatiels due to a staphylococcus infection. It is best treated by restraining the bird, bathing the foot in warm water, drying, draining if necessary, and treating with an antibiotic salve.

Veterinary Help

In all instances where your sick Cockatiel does not respond to your treatment, consult a veterinarian if one knowledgeable in diseases of cage birds is available; otherwise, seek the advice of a more experienced Cockatiel breeder.

References for additional reading: Margaret L. Petrak, *Diseases of Cage and Aviary Birds* (Lea & Febiger, Philadelphia, PA); Arnall & Keymer, *Bird Diseases* (T.F.H. Publications, Neptune City, NJ).

PETS

"All in all, of my whole aviary, containing all kinds and colors, shapes and sizes of birds, I prefer the handsome Cockatiel. I can cheerfully recommend a tame, hand-raised Cockatiel as the perfect house pet—a bird that should be in every home where there is a bird lover. By Bird Lover I mean one who really loves a bird for 'itself' and not just as an ornament for the house, to sit in a pretty cage and accentuate the decorations of a room, or to show it off to friends, but one who wants a bird to love and cherish for its beauty and its cunning ways, and above all for its deep affection to its owner." So wrote Mrs. E. L. Moon in *Experiences with My Cockatiels.*

Marie Olssen, another well-known and experienced aviculturist who dedicated much of her time and love to *Nymphicus hollandicus,* dubbed him: "His Majesty—The Cockatiel."

I know of no one having any experience with Cockatiels who can negate the virtues of Cockies as pets. Their natural intelligence results in a comical and imaginative companion; their affection is lavished on any owner who returns a reasonable amount of attention and love. Each bird's individual personality develops to truly human proportions by association and encouragement. As with a dog that yearns to be in constant physical proximity to its master, one can actually be harassed by the pleading of one's pet when such a guest as Aunt Harriet arrives (she having both a deathly fear of birds and a heart condition). Or perhaps you are hosting a formal dinner for nineteen, resplendent *sans* feathers.

But as individual as every human may be, so too is each Cockie. Some birds will fearlessly approach anyone, some are loyal only unto their owner, some prefer men to women or vice versa, and some are more affectionate than others, more talkative, sassier, or more independent. When respected for whatever their particular quirks may be, they can be very enjoyable company—like Aunt Harriet.

Most birds as a rule dislike being held bodily, i.e., restraining the wings. This is a natural reaction, as it threatens their freedom. However, there are always the trusting exceptions that, despite their instinct, delight in being cuddled and even turned on their backs for a tummy rub. The majority love to have their heads, necks, and chins scratched. Similar behavior can be observed in wild birds as one sidles up to the other, lowers its head and nudges its companion, begging to be preened about the head. At times of molting this is most particularly appreciated, as the shafts on new feathers become prickly and annoying. The bird cannot reach to remove the dried sheaths himself; only through the hit-or-miss scratchings with its foot are they removed. How much more practical and satisfying to have someone else do the job! So delightful, in fact, that the bird will all but fall asleep—eyes closed, crest lowered, and practically cooing.

Jewelry and other such shiny objects are also an irresistible attraction to the playful and curious Cockatiel. My pet Cockatiel, Jelly Bean, has a love affair going with my watch. I have come close to arriving for a dental appointment late or planning dinner early, such is her prowess at manipulating the time stem. And beware, those of you with pierced ears! There is nothing more infuriating to a Cockie than an earring that cannot be deftly swiped and promptly dropped behind the cushion of a chair. Also, should you ever decide to write a letter with a pet Cockatiel on the prowl, you will get no further than a sentence before he or she develops a deep interest in the pen point as it moves across the paper.

For some reason Cockatiels absolutely delight in carrying, pushing, or pulling objects to the side of their cage, table surface, etc., and then hurling the article into space. I recall reading in the English paper, *Cage and Aviary Birds,* about a typical Cockatiel prank. Apparently the author had, with great trouble, obtained two terribly rare and expensive tickets to a game-of-the-century type of sporting event. He had carefully cached them in his desk. When it was time to leave, the tickets were missing. The only credible solution to the mystery was that his pet Cockatiel, who persistently felt it was its duty to houseclean its master's desk, had in customary fashion picked up the tickets, carried them to the edge of the desk, and unerringly hit the wastebasket. Thus a *very* sequestered afternoon was spent by *all*.

Male vs. Female

Before purchasing a pet, one should consider the advantages and disadvantages regarding the sex of the bird. Although hand-fed or newly weaned chicks are easiest to tame, discerning sex is not always possible. If a certain sex is desired and important, then wait for an older bird. At three to six months of age a bird can be accurately sexed and is by no means too old to train.

Males are more apt to talk because they are by nature more vocal than females. Conversely, a hen will be a quieter companion.

In appearance, the Normal and Cinnamon males are prettier than their female counterparts in that they sport the flashier yellow head and more contrasting cheek patches in adult plumage. Lutinos and Pieds, on the other hand, do not have obvious plumage differences between the sexes. In Pearls, the hen alone retains the spotted markings, while the male reverts at maturity to the coloration of a Normal male. In Fallows, the hen sports more yellow suffusion than the cock. Therefore, if appearance is important in the hen, consider one of the last four mutations.

As for differences in personality between the male and female, I have heard more often than not of the hen's disposition as more confiding, affectionate, and easier to train. I have not had many Cockatiel pets myself, but I personally tend to agree. However, there are certainly many owners of male pets who would vehemently disagree. Again, individual personalities and the degree of training might emerge as the real factors if a major survey were taken on this score.

If interest further expands to the point of wanting to breed one's pet, it is usually possible. But realize that you may have to sever some emotional ties for the few months involved.

Household Environment

If perchance you have never been owned by a pet bird before, there are a few healthful and helpful aspects to be considered. A bird in a cage cannot be placed just anywhere. No bird will thrive at floor level. A table top is better, with the best choice being eye level. Be sure that you can always see water and seed needs at a glance, and respect a bird's instinct to perch high.

Do not place a cage next to a door or in a window. Extreme drafts or "cooking" in a hot sun are two sure enemies to a caged bird that cannot move to a more favorable spot when it begins to become uncomfortable. Conversely, do not pamper your pet to the extent that it becomes such a hothouse flower that it wilts at the smallest discomfort. We are discussing Cockatiels, a far hardier bird than many of the more delicate species of caged birds, and they can withstand much lack of consideration, but never for months on end.

Pick a suitable spot and keep the cage there. Even while in a familiar cage, most Cockatiels will not like readjusting constantly to new external surroundings. They are basically homebodies. However, I have heard of people who move their pet each night to their bedroom or other location. Fine, as long as this is a routine and there is not a drastic change in temperature. Always watch for a *continual* heavy molting of feathers. Although you may not feel the differences in temperature and ventilation, a bird which is exposed to a constantly changing environment may naturally react by persistently molting, as his body tries to keep up with the changes. In short, use good judgment. Your pet has only one "outfit." He cannot take off or put on a sweater when needed.

Some people cover their pet's cage every night. This is not usually a necessity, unless nights are particularly cold or drafty. However, covering the cage can at times be a way of discouraging Gremlin the Bird from vocalizing when you specifically wish a quiet moment. Then there are those Carusos who enjoy welcoming the dawn at 5:30 A.M. Their inspiration from a sunrise can handily be postponed a few more hours by covering their "concert hall" before you retire the night before.

Anyone who has raised or had young children around knows that the average house is a stockpile of potentially lethal hazards. So, too, for a pet Cockatiel on the loose. Never leave a pet out of its cage when no one is home! Even a seemingly harmless pot of water in the sink, an open fish tank or toilet, can prove a death trap for a Cockatiel if no lifeguard is on duty. Hot burners or dinner itself on the stove are obvious dangers. Even electrical cords that can be gradually chewed at leisure are an eventual sentence to the "electric chair." Fortunately, paint nowadays cannot by law contain lead, but be aware of painted surfaces on older furniture, window sills, door moldings, etc. A curious and adventurous Cockatiel will inevitably find any hazard your home can harbor. As with an infant or ambulatory child, never let your pet out of your sight when loose, and safely restrain him in his cage when you are away.

Escape!

The usual escapes are through a momentarily opened door or window, or accidentally walking outdoors and forgetting your bird is perched on your shoulder. *Never* assume that because your Cockatiel perpetually stays on your shoulder in the house that he will remain there if you purposely step outside. Crazy as it may sound, I have heard of this happening far too often. It is sad enough to have a pet succumb to natural causes or accident, but to have a beloved pet escape is even more painful, as you may never know what happened to the bird. Frankly, the chances of finding the bird are minimal. A Cockatiel in good condition is a very strong flier in comparison to many birds of comparable size.

When your Cockatiel escapes, it is initially panicked by the strange surroundings. There is no familiar lamp, curtain rod, or cage in sight. It flies high, straight and swiftly, landing only in final desperation, most probably out of sight of home, tired and frightened.

However, for recapture there are a few tricks to try. If within hearing range, he might be directed back home by following the calls of another Cockatiel or by your own familiar voice and phrases. His cage should be placed outside for him to recognize, with food and water placed within to encourage his entering. If the bird is in sight, talking to him while offering favorite treats may help him to return.

As silly as it may sound, the bird may be frightened by the unaccustomed heights, and really does not know how to fly, from 20 feet up, directly down. I have personally observed this on separate occasions when my Hawk-headed Parrot and my mynah bird have escaped. It was the sight of their familiar water dishes that finally encouraged them to overcome their fears. But it took much urging and many attempts, working their way down gradually with each pass. The parrot was no problem to secure once she landed, as she was thoroughly tame. The mynah bird, however, was not hand-tame but finally did land on my head. The water dish was in my outstretched hand, my heart was pounding as I knew I had only one chance to grab the bird before he would be off in a panic. Slowly putting the dish down, I quickly clutched him to my head. It worked, but I feel I was *very* lucky, as both these birds were content to stay in the immediate vicinity for 24 to 36 hours, taking only short flights in the treetops, and were by then very thirsty. Also, they were vocal enough to find; the mynah kept asking the neighbors, "How are you today," and proclaiming, "Stand back, I'm an eagle." I don't know whether I would have been as lucky with a Cockatiel, which tends to be more nervous by nature and might not stick around.

One final shot, literally, would be to drench the bird with water from a hose if he is perched within range. A wet bird cannot fly very well, and will either flutter to the ground in his attempt to fly, or may be retrieved by climbing on a ladder. Again, this is a one-shot deal. If you miss, the bird will take off; or you may have kept him in such A-1 condition that the water merely pours off his well-oiled feathers and he escapes.

By far the best method for ensuring a bird stays in the hand is prevention of escape in the first place.

Feather Clipping

Clipping the wing feathers of a pet bird may prevent escape or at least prevent the bird from getting too far afield to retrieve. This is a measure that should be seriously considered by any pet owner, and not just as a temporary measure for taming the bird initially.

Many people feel it is cruel to hamper the free flight of a bird. But is it cruel to restrict a young child's freedom? Safety is of prime importance. The extent of wing clipping can vary, from almost immobilizing the bird (for taming) to simply inhibiting its flying ability. Clipping is not a permanent measure, for cut feathers will be shed at molt time and will eventually be fully replaced.

Birds seem capable of adjusting to handicaps far more easily than most humans would if similarly incapacitated. I have seen parrots with clipped wings that accepted their temporary handicap so completely that, when their wing feathers had regrown, they seldom, if ever, attempted to fly again.

Quite frankly, I have had no experience with clipped wings. My own pets were all hand-fed youngsters. Wing clipping has also been unnecessary as their chances of an accidental escape are minimal. They reside 99% of the time in the main flights with my "wild" stock, out in the greenhouse. This has proved an ideal arrangement. They remain in top condition with plenty of exercise and constant companionship of their fellows. While they are somewhat less willing to hop on my finger when in the flights (I usually must catch them with a net), once they arrive in the house, they seem to instantly recall the joys of human attention and affection. I urge anyone who can keep their pets in such an arrangement to do so. You will not lose your pet's affection (except during breeding), and your Cockatiel will not have to spend many lonely and boring hours while you are off and running with other commitments.

I have gleaned the following how-tos of wing clipping from my friend and local pet-shop owner, Bill Parlee. It is easier if one person can hold the bird while another does the clipping. If the bird is older, a towel can be used to restrain the bird and avert bites of protest. *Both* wings should be clipped. I have read of clipping only one wing, but have since been advised that this can possibly prove harmful, if not disastrous, to a panicked bird. It expects to fly in a straight line, but can only fly in circles, and thus cannot gauge its landing spot.

Use freshly sharpened scissors. If you will be involved with clipping many wings over the years, you should consider a surgical-quality cutting implement. There are two types of cuts: the Straight and Decline Clips—each has its purpose.

With the Straight Clip, most secondary wing flights and all but the outermost two or three primary wing flights will be cut. All these feathers should be cut just short of the line formed by the secondary and primary wing coverts. This clip will enable the bird to fly straight ahead but not upwards.

The Decline Clip is more severe, and there will be no true flying ability. The bird can only flutter a short distance and strictly in a downward (decline) trajectory. This clip should be considered for taming an older and wilder bird. One should again trim just below the secondary and primary wing coverts but cut *all* the primary flight feathers.

A Normal Cockatiel youngster. Photo by Isabelle Francais.

Immediately after doing either clip, the bird should be released for a test flight. Apparently, there can be a fine line between a clip that allows excessive maneuverability and one that produces immobility. Also remember that on young birds, the flights may still be growing. Within a week or two the bird may regain much of his former flying ability. But an older bird, whose flights have already reached full growth, will remain suitably flightless until the time of his annual molt (usually late summer). Therefore if you clip him in September or October, he might not molt out the cut feathers for almost a year.

A third and more temporary arrangement involves plucking the flight feathers. I had initially thought this ideal, as the bird would regrow the feathers within six weeks time, by then tame. However, considering the large number of flight feathers involved, this must prove quite painful and therefore most distressing to the bird. Pulling a feather here and there for show purposes is one thing. It is similar to pulling a few hairs from your own head, but pulling all hairs from a major area of your head?

Taming

The younger a Cockatiel, the easier he or she is to tame and train. Though it is best to acquire a newly weaned bird, even a youngster three to six months old, which can be more accurately sexed, is still a good candidate for training. It is definitely harder to gain the confidence of a bird a year old or more, but even then it is still not out of the question. At this age, however, the skill of the trainer is more of a factor. If you have never trained a bird before, do not make the attempt with an older bird which may subsequently disappoint you and finally be sentenced to life imprisonment in solitary confinement. Both of you will obviously be disenchanted, but the greater loss will be to the Cockatiel, as he will pay the biggest price for the failure.

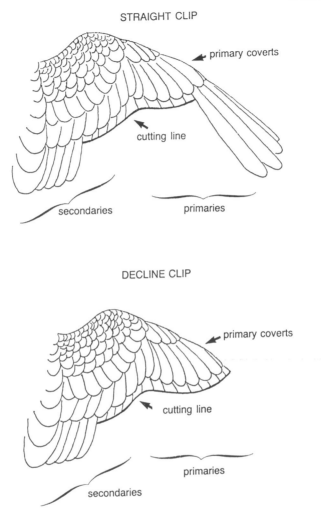

STRAIGHT CLIP

primary coverts

cutting line

secondaries

primaries

DECLINE CLIP

primary coverts

cutting line

primaries

secondaries

There are two basic methods of training. The first is through patience. The bird is brought home and placed in its cage. It will be upset by the change and should be given some time to adjust to its new surroundings and acquaint itself with the strange food and water receptacles. As eager as you are to have this bird fawning over you and reciting Webster's Dictionary, respect its feelings for awhile. If it is upset

Above: A Cinnamon male. Photo by Horst Bielfeld. **Facing page:** A Pied Cream Cockatiel, a very unusual bird! "Cream" is a European term designating a Silver-Cinnamon cross-mutation. Photo by Horst Bielfeld.

with your presence and eagerness, cover the cage partially to give it more security and privacy to ease its adjustment. Simply leave it alone at first.

Be sure you have offered it all or most of the foods to which it was previously accustomed. Because it may be unfamiliar with the new food and water cups, it is wise to scatter seed on the floor to encourage it to eat. It may very likely ignore eating for a day or two, but if it is in good condition, this will not be of consequence.

Gradually it will become accustomed to your proximity; this is a sign to proceed. Talk to it and continue to gain its confidence. If it seems to have certain food preferences, offer them from your fingers through the cage wires (millet spray, greens, etc.). Get the bird accustomed to your hand *gradually* by touching the cage, and eventually by placing your hand gently inside, working toward the bird, and always talking soothingly. It is hard to state a time limit, as how long this will take all depends on the bird and your technique. If the bird shows extreme fear, slow down a bit. However, progress necessitates some initiative on your part. When you reach the stage where you can touch its breast with your finger, try *gently* pushing upwards to unbalance it enough so that it must step onto your finger.

When you finally have the bird finger-trained in the cage, you can consider taking it out of the cage. Anticipate its fright in the "outside" world. Do this at night when the windows will be dark, or draw the curtains or otherwise cover the windows, so that it will not fly into the glass. (This is only a temporary precaution, until the bird becomes tame. Eventually pets become familiar with the area and do not fly into glass windows.) Dim the lights if possible, to further discourage its instinct to fly.

Do not be disheartened should the bird show progress one day and fear the next. Remember, this type of training involves patience. Some birds will respond sooner than others. There are two personalities involved: yours and the bird's. It is said that one can conquer the world with soft talk and patience—it just takes more time. If you are too easily discouraged, you should not acquire an untrained bird. You will be depriving yourself, and more importantly the bird, of a warm and needed relationship to thrive on.

The second method is taming by force. In this instance, the bird must be convinced rather than urged into accepting you as a friend. This should never entail inhumane treatment but only a more forceful approach. The bird must never be indelibly frightened. This method is also more successful with a young bird, as it entails handling of the bird against its wishes. An older bird might inflict its most effective revenge: painful bites. Clipping the wings can be advantageous.

Take the bird into a restricted area (a small room such as a bathroom) where its flight will be limited. Close the curtains and the toilet seat, and dim the lighting. Let the bird loose and retrieve it repeatedly. Initially you will have to catch it bodily, but each time hold it gently, sheltering it against your chest. Talk softly and stroke its back, head, and neck. The bird will eventually realize that this "scratching'" actually feels good and is not a punishment. Gradually loosen your hold, and most probably the bird will take flight once more. This procedure will be repeated again and again, but the bird will tire and eventually can be enticed to climb on your finger rather than having to be picked up bodily. Birds dislike such total restraint of their wings. The sooner you can retrieve the bird without having to grasp it, the sooner it will realize that you are not its enemy. It must learn not to fear your hands.

With a young bird, initial training may require only a fifteen-minute session. On the other hand, depending on your charisma and the bird's stubbornness, it may take several sessions over several days. But remember that when the bird is in your hands, you must be gentle, talk comfortingly, and stroke the bird. Become impatient, even for a moment, and the bird is further convinced that you are not to be trusted and definitely must be avoided at all costs.

Above: A Lutino Pearl fledgling. **Below:** A Golden Pearl nestling. Photos by Mark Runnals.

Above: A Pied Pearl fledgling. Photo by Mark Runnals. **Below:** Underside of the wing of a Normal Cockatiel. Photo by Dr. Herbert R. Axelrod.

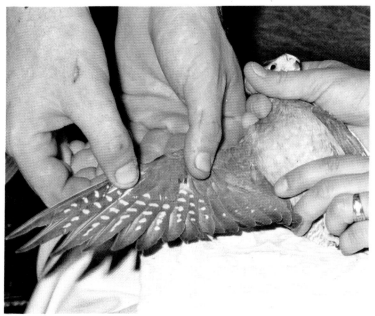

The way to a bird's heart is through its neck, i.e., scratching. Ninety percent of all the pets I have had, Cockies or otherwise, cannot continue battling against such a pleasurable sensation as a neck rub (even wild birds entice their own mates into similar preening behavior). Eventually you will find your pet begging for such attention by lowering its head and urging you to scratch it.

Finally, once your pet is tame, do not make the mistake of allowing it to become accustomed to such constant freedom that he does not consider its cage a home. The happy medium is a bird that enjoys its outings, but will return to its cage for food and shelter by *choice*. A standard routine can achieve this; set aside only specified times each day for flying. It is amazing how time-oriented a bird can become through habit—feeding times, flight times, and bedtimes. You would swear such birds harbor a pocket watch beneath their wings. Such a trained and disciplined pet is a joy to own, as it in effect does not own you.

Talking

Yes, Cockatiels can be taught to talk. However, if this feature is your *main* reason for obtaining a pet, you might be happier with investing in an African Grey, Double Yellow-head, or Yellow-naped Amazon parrot, or even a mynah bird, as these are considered more consistently the top avian talkers.

I tend to be a bit short with people whose main concern when considering a Cockatiel hinges on the bird's ability to talk. Novices seem to think this is the main purpose of owning a psittacine bird. In truth, this is only an added feature; like having air conditioning in your car or a self-cleaning oven. By far the most important aspect of a pet bird is its personality (the car for transportation, and the oven for cooking).

The first bird I ever owned was a tame Budgie who spent the major part of his life with me at college. He truthfully should have graduated with a *summa cum laude* in English, as his vocabulary would have put a few parrots to shame (as well as a few ministers). As I sit here now, 25 years later, I can still run through his entire repertoire of phrases, which included entire poems and songs, after the thousands of times that I recited them in order. He could talk for minutes at a stretch, beginning with his first learned phrase "pretty bird," all the way through to the complete chorus of "Birds Do It, Bees Do It" (which ended in a rather obscene phrase that my roommate was persistent enough to impress upon his memory).

Dear Tweety eventually lived out his life, and it was a few years before I could even think of another bird. But when I did, I figured I would go to the Rolls Royce of talking birds: an African Grey. I wrote Bill Wilson at Norshore Pets in Illinois, stating my wish. His reply I have repeated many times since: No, he did not have a Grey at the moment, but he did have one heck of a tame Hawk-headed Parrot. No, the species was not noted for talking, but this bird was a pet with a capital *P*.

I have since acquired an African Grey and a mynah bird, both of which *do* talk up a storm. But Peanuts, my Hawk-head (who incidentally ended up saying "pretty bird" and "hello," albeit as though he had marbles in his mouth), was nevertheless Number One of the whole roost for ten wonderful years. Unfortunately, he died in a freak accident, and we miss him dearly.

A talking pet usually requires a great deal of patience and persistence on the owner's part, and I no longer think it worthwhile. However, as long as the importance of the bird's talking is kept in proper perspective, it is a subject that should be discussed. A Cockatiel's ability to mimic should not be altogether discredited. It is a natural trait, and a further consideration and extension of the bird's potential.

Remember that, just as in humans, the gift for gab can vary according to the individual. There is no sure way of picking a potential talker, but often a proven vocalizing pet, when bred, will be more likely to pass the inclination on to his offspring. Usually males are considered more appropriate

Above: A Cinnamon male Cockatiel courting a Cinnamon hen. Photo by Nancy A. Reed.

Facing page: In Europe, a bird such as this is called a "Banded" Pied, in reference to the white collar. Photo by Horst Bielfeld.

students, because they are by nature more vocal than female birds. However, this is not to say that hens can't or won't talk, but that they are generally less likely to mimic.

A story that contradicts this involves my original pair of Cockatiels. Both were completely wild breeders. One day I put my daughter's pet Cockatiel out in the flights for exercise and a change of environment. He was frightened by the unfamiliar surroundings and only clung to the wires, repeating frantically, "Pretty bird, pretty bird." After a time I could see he was not going to take advantage of what I thought would be a welcome switch from his humdrum routine, and I retrieved him. Would you believe that the next morning I was out feeding the aviary birds, and suddenly I heard, "Pretty bird, pretty bird"? My wild hen Cockatiel had picked up the phrase to perfection in 24 hours! So much for discounting the prowess of a female. But yes, males, being more vocal, are most inclined to mimic.

One's first inclination is to teach the "wolf whistle." And this of course is the easiest sound for your bird to pick up. It is closest to his mode of speech. But resist the temptation, at least to begin with, as the bird may become so proficient as to feel there is no need to progress further in breaking down the language barrier between you and him. You might end up with a bird that wolf whistles 92 times a minute, on command or impromptu. (This might be fun to begin with, but it becomes tedious after ten years!)

At the beginning, only one person should endeavor to teach the chosen phrase. If several people are repeating the phrase, the bird will find it confusing. He is not only trying to pronounce the words, he attempts to imitate the *tone* of voice as well. (Usually a woman's voice is easier for a Cockatiel to simulate.) Once the initial breakthrough of the first words is made, different people can teach his or her own chosen phrase. The first mimicry can take weeks or months, but less and less time will then be needed to learn new words. It all depends on the individual bird and the persistence of the teacher.

In choosing the first phrase, be aware that hard consonants are easiest for the bird to imitate—thus the usual "pretty bird" with its *p, t, b,* and *d.* "How are you" would come out less distinct, until the bird becomes more proficient.

Speak loudly and clearly. The bird will imitate what it hears. If you whisper, it will whisper even more quietly. While it could never shout, due to its size, it can speak with adequate gusto if imitating a well-projected phrase. Also, birds are apt to speak more rapidly than humans. By accentuating pronunciation very distinctly, it will slow down your verbal presentation of the phrase, and the bird will not slur the sounds.

Just as with children and other humans, the bird must be paying attention for best results. If it is fiddling with a toy or more involved with observing activities outside its cage, it might be best to remove such toys and cover three sides of its cage, or both, during lesson time. However, during "recess," a mirror in the cage may further encourage it to practice talking as it tries to communicate with and impress its reflection.

There are also records on the market which repeat a specific phrase. For that matter, you can make a tape of your own chosen saying, and then leave the house during the time that it is playing to safeguard your sanity.

I honestly can't say from personal experience whether such methods will effectively train a bird. Back in the days of my pet Budgie, I played such a record, but I think I out-performed its repetition with my own phrases, and Tweety never did learn the expressions presented by the disc. Perhaps the stimulus of the words coming from the pet bird's "Almighty in Person" may be more conducive, meaningful, and stimulating in the long run.

Finally, single birds generally make better students. When two or more birds congregate, they prefer discussions among themselves and are less apt to include your foreign tongue in the conversation.

Above: Whiteface Cockatiels, male and female. Photo by Dale R. Thompson and George D. Dodge.

Facing page: Close-up of a Normal male Cockatiel. Photo by Horst Bielfeld.

Left: Cockatiel youngsters on a playground. Photo by Isabelle Francais.

PREPARATIONS FOR BREEDING

Often so much interest is generated by a single pet that the natural progression is to further one's knowledge—and fun—through breeding. What an exciting experience it is when that first egg not only appears but eventually hatches. Experiencing the miracle of life as the tiny chick grows, then finally becomes an independent new Cockie in the world, carries the reward of feeling that you were a very important part of the whole process. Congratulations!—you must have done something right!

Unfortunately, however, your first, or fourth, or even fifteenth attempt may not be all that rosy. Birds are not machines. They can be as unpredictable as the weather (and sometimes it is the weather that becomes the fatal factor). The full cycle from first mating to a weaned chick takes about eleven weeks, and that allows lots of time for something to go wrong. I am constantly amazed that a chick ever survives to sing its own tune. Here lies the challenge and hoped-for reward in breeding birds (plus the less esoteric, but decidedly more practical, monetary reward that sales will bring to your seed-and-feed budget).

Pairing
It is not true that all Cockatiels pair for life, although some pairs are as devoted to their mates as a pet is to its owner. If one dies, the other sometimes will mourn for a long time. But some birds are downright fickle! I have a male that bred one year with two hens, and they all raised their young together in one nest box. One hen was a week or so behind the

other in laying her eggs. Only one of her eggs hatched, the rest were lost in the madness; but she pitched in and fed the first hen's babies as she would her own.

Pet birds can be induced to breed successfully, but, I would be dubious about a Cockatiel that has been your constant companion for years and truly does not know it is anything but human. Also, many people fear losing their pet's affection. Granted, during the breeding period, he or she will be less endeared to you, perhaps even aggressive, but when through breeding, the bird will probably return to his or her former ways.

Mrs. Moon swore by hand-tamed birds for breeders. I have found this valid in that they are much steadier. They are far less likely to puncture or break their eggs in panic or desert their young, and will go about their business despite your nose being ever present. However, "wild" birds usually will quiet down once they become used to you and your routine or, when paired to a tame mate, will follow his or her example to a degree.

A Cockatiel is mature enough to breed between the ages of one and two years. I have had both male and female successfully raise young at eight months of age. A friend has had fertile eggs from six-month-old birds. These are exceptions, and a young bird should not be condemned if no interest is shown in breeding, eggs are not fertile, or the young are not properly fed. With some birds, breeding seems to be learned from experience. It is often better to pair an experienced bird with a virgin breeder. This eliminates a lot of fumbling around. If the young bird should become slack in his or her responsibilities, the older will often take over and set the example. I've seen a hen incubate 24 hours a day. When the chicks hatched, the young male accepted his role, and both fed and raised the young. On the second clutch, he fulfilled his egg-sitting duties properly. However, with no alternative, or with an important reason for the cross, I've had pairings of virgin birds run quite smoothly.

Left: A Lutino Cockatiel being offered a treat from the hand, which helps to win its confidence. Photo by Isabelle Francais.

Facing page: A Silver male—in this picture the eyes do not appear red. Photo by Horst Bielfeld.

Below: A Cinnamon youngster that shows the telltale white blotches on the back of the head indicating that it is split for Pied. Photo by Horst Bielfeld.

On the other hand, when is a bird too old? In my research, I found records of a pair that were both twelve years old, another fourteen, and finally a male of nineteen still going strong!

Should mutations be paired together (Lutino to Lutino, Pied to Pearl, etc.)? Two large, strong, preferably not closely related birds, can produce fine specimens as if outcrossed to Normals or split Normals. But the aim should not be to simply mass-produce a rarer and more expensive mutation. Please develop and improve the strain.

With some established mutations such as the Lutino, Pearl, and Cinnamon, fertility and productivity seem to be as good as with Normals. Some breeders debate that the Pieds are less reliable. One fault which is often accentuated by breeding Lutino to Lutino is the unsightly bald spot on the head, and sometimes on the shoulder joints. This must be eliminated by careful selection of the Lutinos to be paired, or by crossing with Normals.

In other words, pair your birds for a reason! Your aim might be to improve on size and conformation, color or pattern, or pairing birds so that they can be sexed in the nest. Or perhaps you would like to produce young that would make exceptional pets: choose parents that have been fine pets themselves, or birds that are naturally steady and show a flair for mimicking.

However, what one works out on paper does not always suit the birds set up to breed. This can be maddening when you have a super reason for the pairing! Sometimes it is simply that one of the pair has not reached breeding condition yet. Time and diet may solve the disparity. Usually, if a male and female have reached peak breeding condition, any mate looks good!

Privacy
Curb your curiosity. Some birds will tolerate your big nose in their nest box every two hours (if they are steady or tame), but sometimes the best rule is to keep your hands off. I know

how anxious you will be to know how many eggs there are, or if any chicks have hatched, etc. If a pair is totally unfamiliar with you, check the nest box only when both are out of the nest (which is seldom). It is important that your birds become accustomed to at least a daily check of the nest box. This might prevent an unnecessary fatality. Usually as a pair gets further along in their incubational duties or feeding, they become less flighty and more defensive of their clutch. Use discretion and expediency in such cases.

Cage or Flight?
For successful breeding, we must house the birds in a cage or flight situated in an area that will be as free as possible from disturbance. The living room or the kitchen would not be wise choices. In most homes there is too much activity involved in these rooms. Also, you would be constantly sweeping up feathers and seed husks. Parent birds go through an astonishing amount of seed! A spare room, cellar, garage, or outside flight would be more private and less necessary to keep free of hulls and feathers. Also, space must be allotted for all the young when weaned.

Most of us do not have extensive areas within the house to convert to spacious flights, nor perhaps a yard or climate to make outdoor aviaries feasible. Evaluate the area available and keep in mind that the success in breeding and raising robust young seems most often to be in direct proportion to the size of the flight. You will do better, in the long run, to work with only one or two pairs in a smaller area than with more birds that must be squeezed in like books on a shelf. Plan for one or two good-sized flights and one or two smaller flights (or large cages) for breeding. The larger flights are necessary for the birds to exercise and reach peak condition when not breeding, and for the young. Pet birds of course can get exercise in their out-of-cage times, so a flight is not necessary. During the breeding season, the pairs can be put in smaller quarters, if necessary, as they are less active while incubating and feeding.

Above: A pair of Lutino Cockatiels, both outstanding birds in immaculate condition. Photo by Bill Parlee.

Facing page: A Cinnamon Pearl female with very attractive and unusual coloration. On the show bench, however, it would be considered too extreme: the Pearl markings are so extensive that they almost mask the contrasting Cinnamon coloration. Show standards call for a balance when mutations are combined. Photo by Horst Bielfeld.

Cockatiels set up for colony breeding. Photo by Tony Barrett.

Specifically, what size should a flight cage be? Larger than a bread box, although I've seen others' birds breed in cages about as small! The largest of my four big flights measures about 10′ in length, 4′ wide, and 9′ high. I use this as a general flight, but have also had some success in housing in it two compatible breeding pairs. My four smallest breeding flights are 4′ long, 2′ wide, and 3′ high. I consider this the minimum size to which I would ever subject the birds. Although the dimensions have proven adequate, I truly wish I had space for 20′ flights for all purposes.

Colony Breeding
I mentioned breeding two pairs in a flight. Housing two or more pairs together is called "colony breeding." Many breeders have claimed successful results with this system. One must obviously use a flight proportional in size to the num-

ber of pairs. I personally find too many faults with the practice. For one, there is no control as to who breeds with whom unless previously mated birds are used (they are most apt to pair up again). Also, no matter how compatible the pairs are, the whole cycle is slower. Rather than taking about eleven weeks from mating to the time the young are weaned, it will run longer; if two clutches are to be raised, the birds will be working for well over six months. However, there is the valid consideration that if a group of birds are let loose and can choose their own mates, they "work" better as a team. Weigh the pros and cons, but for "planned parentage," colony breeding is impractical. Overall, I have had better success with one pair to a flight.

Breeding Season
Unlike Canaries and various other bird species, Cockatiels do not have a set breeding season. This is very helpful, as one can plan according to one's own lifestyle. I like to set most of my pairs up in December. In our family, January and February are the least busy months, and there is more time to spend on the newly hatched birds. Also, this gives the birds six months (for two clutches) before the weather gets uncomfortably warm. They finish up in June and have time to recuperate before their molt in July and August. Furthermore, the young are filled-out and in fine feather for the shows in October and November. Finally, it leaves me the busy holidays in December (while they are incubating) to spend with my family. This schedule of the breeding cycle works best for me. But you can breed anytime, as long as a good two months following breeding are allotted for the molt. Those with outdoor aviaries are governed more by the weather and will have to commence breeding when conditions are favorable.

Out of Season
I prefer to separate my males and females when not breeding, placing them in larger cock or hen pens for a deserved

Above: A lovely photo of a Silver male showing the underwing feather arrangement. Photo by Horst Bielfeld.

Facing page: Without being able to see the redness in the eyes, this young Pied Silver male could be mistaken for simply a Pied. Photo by Horst Bielfeld.

Left: Two birds on an opened nest box. Photo by Isabelle Francais.

rest and recuperation. This makes it easier to re-pair birds to different mates if you did not like the results of the previous year's nesting. Also, young males will not become attached to "unsuitable" females.

If a particular pair has proven themselves with quality young, they need not be separated, but should be moved from the breeding quarters to a larger flight. Even if separated, they will most probably remate. On the other hand, my original pair of Cockies, who had bred well for two years, apparently "divorced" the third year. I had set the male up with his original "wife," but all he wanted was his daughter in the adjoining flight. I finally gave in, and he and his choice raised thirteen beautiful big babies in two clutches in four months—a good argument for allowing males to pick their own mates.

Occasionally one will have a male that comes into breeding condition too early and, if aggressive by nature, may raise a ruckus in the cock pen. It is best to separate him from the others. His harassment can wear them down. Also, such a male cannot be used in colony breeding, as he would get too upset by other birds in the vicinity of his nest box.

Breeding Limitations

Allow a pair to raise only two broods per year. Two clutches of four or more young are plenty of work for a pair. Don't get greedy! If you have hand-fed a clutch, or if only two or three young were raised per nest, or they goofed a nest, then possibly a third sitting can be considered. A good feeding pair works very hard raising their young. Just hand-feed a few babies and you will have great respect for those parents.

Don't overbreed your pair. Aside from it being detrimental to their health, the following year they may be useless. It is not worth it in the long run. Although it is exasperating to throw out a clutch of eggs that are laid and incubated while the parents are weaning their second batch, if you can't foster the eggs, you must dispose of them.

COLOR MUTATIONS AND BREEDING EXPECTATIONS

by Dr. Rainer R. Erhart

The Advent of Novelty

The history of aviculture is filled with interesting anecdotes of bird keeping by emperors and kings, the exploration and capture of exotic birds in faraway places, and first-breeding successes of birds imported to various collections in Europe and North America.

However, few of these events can rival the excitement and the initial secrecy once a new and colorful mutation has appeared in someone's aviary. In fact, I can safely say that the real interest in any species, be it poultry, pigeon, Canary, Zebra Finch, Budgerigar, or Cockatiel, has come only after the arrival of some interesting new color varieties.

It is difficult to guess why a new mutation is so attractive to a breeder, but I am sure it is partly because of the uniqueness of such an event. Who wouldn't want to be the first to own an all-black Budgerigar, a bright red lovebird or an orange Cockatiel? To date none of these mutations have as yet appeared, but wouldn't it be exciting to find one of these little jewels in your nest box?

A second reason why new mutations are so keenly sought is that breeding success can bring the new owner a financial boost or, at the very least, desirable terms in trading for other valuable birds. To give you an idea of some past events, let us only consider the very first blue Budgerigars. It is said that prices offered for them in England were equal to those of the finest race horses. In our own country, the first white Cockatiels fetched prices of more than $1,000 in the early

A Normal male Cockatiel. Photo by Horst Bielfeld.

sixties, and the Albino Ringnecks until very recently have carried a price tag of about $5,000.

The glamour of new mutations doesn't always end in a big pot of gold. New mutations often prove to be somewhat delicate, and many a new color has quickly disappeared again because the owner failed to establish a viable strain. The Lutino Plumhead Parakeet is a good case in point. This very attractive mutation has occurred on several occasions, but no one has ever successfully established it.

I have been asked many times, even by some quite serious breeders, "How did you produce your first White (or Pearl, or Cinnamon) Cockatiel?" The implication here is that I used some magic formula or some shades of gray or white to produce a new color. Generally, color mutations occur accidentally in someone's aviary without the person really trying. It is your happy task to locate such mutations and, with some luck, acquire one or more of the offspring. A new mutation in the hands of an experienced breeder who has some basic knowledge of avian genetics may then lead to the establishment of this new color.

Most breeders feel very uncomfortable with the subject of genetics, and after having glanced through a great number of books dealing with avian inheritance, I cán finally understand why. Most commentaries are more difficult to follow than our dreaded tax forms; hence most people give up after the first few paragraphs. I am not sure that my exposition will be any simpler, but after having introduced some of the necessary terms, I will try to simply list some of the expectations, rather than letting you work and struggle with all possibilities. I do want to caution, however, that some sex-linked Cockatiel cross-mutations are the result of crossing-over, and the rates of crossing-over have not been fully documented.

General Description
Four "standard" Cockatiel mutations are presently recognized at major bird shows in the United States. They are the Pied, Lutino, Pearl, and Cinnamon. Other mutations such as

the Whiteface, Albino, Fallow, and Silvers are usually rele-
gated to the Rare Variety section, because of the fewer entries
with these more recent mutations. With time we shall see
more mutations and combinations, possibly at an accelerated
rate, as has been the case with Budgerigars, Zebra Finches,
and lovebirds.

Pied

Pieds originated in the U.S. in the mid-forties and can best
be described as a "patchwork quilt." No two are alike, but
the most desirable and most expensive birds are those with
heavy and evenly pied markings. The saddle-back pied is a
good example of an evenly marked, heavily pied bird.

Of all the Cockatiel mutations, the Pieds are the most difficult to sex. Usually one must rely on telltale male behavior.
But once you have a devoted pair, it is fun to breed them
because each nestling is marked just a bit differently. There
is also general agreement among breeders that Pieds are the
least reliable parents and that losses of young birds are higher
than in any of the other mutations. There is no good statisti-
cal evidence, but my own observations tend to confirm such
a claim.

Finally, Pieds tend to have a greater suffusion of yellow
pigments, giving them a very attractive appearance. In England, the terms Primrose Pieds and Buttercup Pieds have
been established to differentiate between light and deep yellow Pieds.

Lutino

Before discussing this very attractive and widely kept mutation, we must have some background as to its proper name.
When the first of these mutations appeared in 1958 they were
referred to as Albinos, retaining that name until the early
seventies. At that time someone decided that since this bird,
with its yellow crest and red cheek patches, still retains the
carotenoid pigments, it really wasn't a true Albino and therefore ought to be called a Lutino. This renaming created some

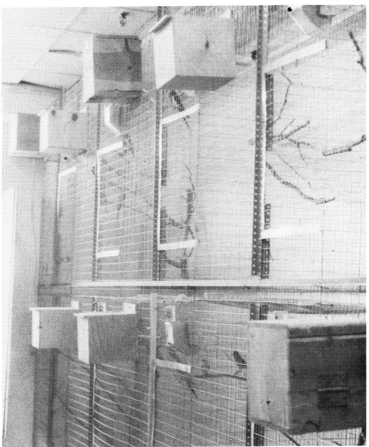

Section of an indoor flight set-up. Photo by Bill Parlee.

confusion and resulted in numerous terms, including Albino, Lutino, White, Ino, and Cream Albino. All are found in the literature to describe the same mutation. Today, most books refer to this mutation as Lutino.

In aviculture an Albino is a red-eyed, pure white bird that lacks *all* pigments (melanins and carotenoids). A Lutino, on

131

the other hand, is a red-eyed buttercup-yellow bird in which only the dark pigments (melanins) are missing. By these definitions, our white Cockatiel is neither an Albino nor a Lutino since it is neither pure white nor is it buttercup yellow. However, it is important to remember that, since all melanins are lacking and only the carotenoids are present, we do have a lutinistic bird even though the feathers are basically white or yellowish white.

Because Lutinos come in many shades of yellow, from nearly white to a deep yellow, I would recommend a system of description similar to the British one. A very pale yellow bird is simply a Lutino; one with a medium yellow is a Primrose Lutino, and a deep yellow bird is a Buttercup Lutino. This description would clearly differentiate a Cream Lutino from a buttercup-yellow Lutino, which already graces some aviaries.

A final note to those who prefer the term *Albino*. Basically, you also have a valid argument, because in science all organisms which lack part or all of their melanistic pigments are albinotic. Geneticists don't even acknowledge the term *lutino*, and thus you won't find it in the genetic literature. But if you want to be active in aviculture, perhaps you ought to see the aviculturist's point of view as well.

Let us now return to the history and description of the Lutino mutation. It first appeared in 1958 in Mr. Barringer's aviaries in Florida. At first little progress was made, but when Mrs. Moon acquired some of Mr. Barringer's stock, it took only a few years before her strain of "Moonbeams" was well established. Mrs. Moon, who was an accomplished breeder of psittacine birds, tells about her first Albinos, as she called them, in an interesting article published in the *American Cage-Bird Magazine* (Aug. 1968).

The Lutino Cockatiel is one of the most beautiful of all the Cockatiel mutations. All have dark red eyes, yellow head and crest, bright red cheek patches, and predominantly creamy white feathers on the rest of the body and flights. Hens tend to be more yellow, particularly with age.

Until 1968, Mrs. Moon's price tag for the Cream Lutinos was $750 a pair. Prices peaked at about $1,000 a pair when European breeders competed for this attractive newcomer. This is typical of all new mutations—an example of supply and demand. In the many years since the Cream Lutino occurred, the price has naturally dropped considerably as stock became more plentiful.

Pearl

In the mid-sixties a new, speckled mutation appeared in a West German collection and was generally known as the Pearl Cockatiel. But is also appeared under the names Scaly, Laced, Pearled, and Opaline.

This is the "Dalmatian" of Cockatiel mutations, bearing an array of spots—specifically, each feather is centrally spotted or outlined in yellow or white. Yellow pearled birds are often referred to as Golden Pearls, while the white pearled birds are known as Silver Pearls. The pearls are most evident on the head, shoulders, wings, and back of the bird, the amount varying with individuals. A photograph gives the best description. This mutation is unique in that the male Pearl loses his spots as he matures; if not after the first molt, by the second year he appears to be a Normal male. This makes banding a necessity, as he is, of course, still a pure Pearl when breeding. In time, we hope to breed Pearls in which the male maintains the pearls as well. Some Pearls have developed so much white or yellow edging on their feathers that they are called Lacewings, or Laced Cockatiels.

Cinnamon

Chronologically, the Cinnamon (or Isabel) is next, having been first observed in Belgium in the late sixties. This is a very attractive bird, although some have described it somewhat accurately but decidedly not very flatteringly as a Normal which has been in the sun too long. It is a pastel brown-gray with the same dimorphic coloring of an adult Normal. Again, individuals vary, but preference is for the lighter, creamy tan color. Whereas, on the one hand, a deep gray-black Normal is striking because of contrast, I think the softness of the Cinnamon—i.e., the close blending of fawn, white, and yellow—is a harmonious treat.

Fallow

Quite similar to the Cinnamons but distinctly more delicate in color are the Fallows. They sport very light pastel buff-yellow colors, particularly the females, and their eyes are visibly red. In most recent literature the Fallows have been incorrectly lumped together with the Silvers. Though they don't really look much alike, too many ambiguous descriptions have led people to believe Fallows and Silvers are one in the same mutation.

Silver

One of the least common of all Cockatiel mutations is the Silver. No one seems to be quite sure when it first appeared, but there is good evidence that the Silver was first bred in Belgium in the late fifties. Then, for almost ten years, no one saw it again until the late sixties, when prices offered for this mutation reached astronomical figures.

The basic body color of this mutation is a beautiful metallic silver-gray. The eyes are bright red and, along with the orange cheek patches, give good contrast between the light gray and yellow feathers of the head. Silver is a recessive mutation. David West of California has been particularly devoted to establishing this mutation in the U.S.

Whiteface and Albino

The history and descriptions of these varieties have been treated in an earlier chapter.

Other Color Varieties

Before closing this section we should at least mention some other mutations or color phases that have been occasionally observed. Perhaps the most controversial of these are the

Black-eyed Whites. They look exactly like Lutinos but have black instead of dark red eyes. To differentiate between them one has to almost view them in sunlight; only then can one identify the slight difference in eye color. When they were first noticed in Europe, they were thought to be a simple recessive mutation; and when they were subsequently mated with the sex-linked Lutinos, the genetics became so hopelessly confused that the Black-eyed White nearly disappeared. Some Black-eyed Whites have also surfaced in the U.S. and are usually known as Bull's-eyes. Bull's-eyes are usually raised from very heavily pied birds, which eventually results in all clear, black-eyed birds. Naturally, these birds are recessive, but one can always expect some pied birds when mating clear Pied to clear Pied.

Occasionally, one also comes across a very darkly pigmented Cockatiel, a color phase which has been achieved through selection. Mrs. Moon, for example, had for many years tried to breed dark-to-dark and light-to-light, hoping to eventually end up with a bird as black as a crow. I recently saw a nearly black Cockatiel in a European aviary.

For years some white birds have shown orange lacings, but again, no one has been able to maintain these markings through selection. It seems to be a modification rather than a mutation.

Green Cockatiels have also been reported from time to time. The green in all cases is not a vivid parrot green, but mostly a light green-yellowish cast. It is interesting that most of these greenish birds have extremely loose and often abnormally long body feathers. It is possible that the new feather structure is actually contributing to new and different refractive properties which produce the greenish sheen. Mr. Morris in California is currently trying to establish a good strain of this mutation.

Basic Genetic Terms

There is little doubt that the successful breeder of a new mutation also must have some basic knowledge of genetics. Unfortunately, there are very few people motivated enough to teach themselves even the most elementary genetic principles. This reluctance to learn the "rules" often reminds me of kids with simple arithmetic problems. They have a mental block, and they tell themselves they just can't do it. Once you have a similar block for genetic principles, it seems that not even the best writing will make the slightest dent, because you will simply skip over that part of the chapter, wishing for an easy summary at the end. Well, I have succumbed to these wishes and have produced tables summarizing the breeding expectations for most of the various Cockatiel mutations.

Before we progress to these tables, however, there are a few basic definitions and concepts that all readers should remember. Geneticists often talk about *genes,* because they carry all the factors of inheritance, including body shape and size, the color of eyes, skin, or feathers, brain size and complexity, etc. Each gene is located at a very specific place within a *chromosome,* which is a rod-shaped body located within the nucleus of the cell. The important thing for us to remember is that each complex organism has an even number of chromosomes, and that half of them contain the factors inherited from the male, while the other half carry those from the female. In other words, during the process of fertilization, all the factors of inheritance from the male are combined with those of the female. Some of these factors are *dominant,* others are *recessive.* If, for example, we breed a Normal Cockatiel with a Pied Cockatiel, then all offspring will look gray (Normal) but will carry the Pied factor invisibly. Therefore we say that Normal is dominant, while Pied is recessive. To date, all Cockatiel mutations are recessive to Normal, though we differentiate between simple recessives and sex-linked recessives.

In simple recessive mutations, the genes are located on the chromosomes known as autosomes. The sex-linked genes, on the other hand, are found on a sex chromosome, and therefore the color is related to the sex of the bird. In Cockatiels, the simple recessive mutations are Pied, Silver, Fallow, and Whiteface. The sex-linked recessives are Lutino, Cinnamon, and Pearl.

Every species of bird in the wild has its own characteristic feather colors. A wild Budgerigar is basically green, and so are lovebirds, ringnecked parakeets, etc. The wild form of the Cockatiel, on the other hand, is gray. Sometimes an accident of nature produces a sudden color change, which occurs in the genes. Such a spontaneous change is referred to as a *mutation*. A bird which carries a mutant gene but doesn't actually show the mutant color is said to be *split* for that color. For example, in a previous paragraph we mentioned a cross between Normal and a Pied Cockatiel, and all offspring looked Normal. Well, even though they looked Normal, they were still split (heterozygous) for Pied. Proper pairings would eventually give us some birds that looked Pied.

Finally, we have a process called *crossing-over*. During this process, pieces of a pair of chromosomes break off and exchange places. Such crossovers have occurred when we pair two sex-linked recessive mutations in Cockatiels. Here, two or more color factors have ended up on one sex chromosome, which means that two or more colors (such as Pearl and Cinnamon) appear on the same bird. It is not known exactly at what rates crossing-over occurs in Cockatiels, but breeders have found the crossover rate for Lutino × Pearl to be about 50%. Crossover rates for other sex-linked factors may be lower. Table VI gives breeding expectations once crossing-over has occurred.

Tables of Expectations

Even though there are only a handful of Cockatiel mutations, the number of crosses which can be attempted is very large. I have tried to summarize the basic crosses in the following tables.

In using these tables it should always be kept in mind that the percentages are based on a very large sample. Just as a family of four children doesn't always end up with two boys and two girls, so your birds in one, two, or even three nests will not come out exactly as predicted by the tables. The tables are simply a guide to a scientific approach to bird breeding; the outcome may not always be to your liking.

Table I: Recessive Mutations: Pied, Silver, Fallow, Whiteface

"Splits" are indicated by the slash; thus "Normal /Pied" is read "Normal split for Pied." Though Pied was chosen for the example, Silver, Fallow, or Whiteface may be substituted for Pied, and the results will remain the same. For instance, Normal × Silver = 100% Normal /Silver.

Normal × Normal = 100% Normal
Normal × Pied = 100% Normal /Pied
Normal × Normal /Pied = 50% Normal; 50% Normal /Pied
Normal /Pied × Normal /Pied = 25% Normal; 50% Normal /Pied; 25% Pied
Pied × Normal /Pied = 50% Pied; 50% Normal /Pied
Pied × Pied = 100% Pied

Table II: Recessive Mutations Crossed with Recessive Mutations

Though Silver and Pied were chosen for the example, Fallow or Whiteface may be substituted where Silver or Pied appears.

Silver × Pied = 100% Normal /Silver /Pied
Silver × Normal /Silver /Pied = 25% Normal /Silver; 25% Normal /Silver /Pied; 25% Silver /Pied; 25% Silver
Silver × Normal /Pied = 50% Normal /Silver; 50% Normal /Silver /Pied
Normal /Silver /Pied × Pied = 25% Normal /Pied; 25% Normal /Pied /Silver; 25% Pied; 25% Pied /Silver
Normal /Silver /Pied × Normal /Silver /Pied = 6.25% Normal; 25% Normal /Silver /Pied; 12.5% Normal /Pied; 12.5% Normal /Silver; 6.25% Pied; 12.5% Pied /Silver; 12.5% Silver /Pied; 6.25% Silver; 6.25% Pied Silver

Normal /Silver /Pied × Normal /Pied = 12.5% Normal; 25% Normal /Pied; 12.5% Pied; 12.5% Normal /Silver; 25% Normal /Pied /Silver; 12.5% Pied /Silver

Table III: Sex-linked Mutations: Lutino, Pearl, Cinnamon

Though Lutino was chosen for the example, Pearl or Cinnamon may be substituted for Lutino.

Normal ♂ × Normal ♀ = 50% Normal ♂; 50% Normal ♀

Normal ♂ × Lutino ♀ = 50% Normal /Lutino ♂; 50% Normal ♀

Normal /Lutino ♂ × Normal ♀ = 25% Normal ♂; 25% Normal /Lutino ♂; 25% Normal ♀; 25% Lutino ♀

Normal /Lutino ♂ × Lutino ♀ = 25% Normal /Lutino ♂; 25% Lutino ♂; 25% Normal ♀; 25% Lutino ♀

Lutino ♂ × Normal ♀ = 50% Normal /Lutino ♂; 50% Lutino ♀

Lutino ♂ × Lutino ♀ = 50% Lutino ♂; 50% Lutino ♀

Table IV: Sex-linked Mutations Crossed with Recessive Mutations

Though Pied and Pearl were chosen for this example, Lutino and Cinnamon may be substituted for Pearl, and Silver, Fallow, or Whiteface for Pied.

Pearl ♂ × Pearl ♀ = 50% Pearl ♂; 50% Pearl ♀

Pearl ♂ × Pied ♀ = 50% Normal /Pearl /Pied ♂; 50% Pearl /Pied ♀

Pearl ♂ × Normal /Pied ♀ = 25% Normal /Pearl ♂; 25% Normal /Pearl /Pied ♂; 25% Pearl ♀; 25% Pearl /Pied ♀

Pearl ♂ × Pearl /Pied ♀ = 25% Pearl ♂; 25% Pearl /Pied ♂; 25% Pearl ♀; 25% Pearl /Pied ♀

Pearl ♂ × Pied Pearl ♀ = 50% Pearl /Pied ♂; 50% Pearl /Pied ♀

Pied ♂ × Pearl ♀ = 50% Normal /Pearl /Pied ♂; 50% Normal /Pied ♀

Pied ♂ × Pied ♀ = 50% Pied ♂; 50% Pied ♀

Pied ♂ × Normal /Pied ♀ = 25% Normal /Pied ♂; 25% Pied ♂; 25% Normal /Pied ♀; 25% Pearl ♀

Pied ♂ × Pearl /Pied ♀ = 25% Pied /Pearl ♂; 25% Normal /Pearl /Pied ♂; 25% Pied ♀; 25% Normal /Pied ♀

Pied ♂ × Pied Pearl ♀ = 50% Pied /Pearl ♂; 50% Pied ♀

Normal /Pearl ♂ × Pearl ♀ = 25% Pearl ♂; 25% Normal /Pearl ♂; 25% Pearl ♀; 25% Normal ♀

Normal /Pearl ♂ × Pied ♀ = 25% Normal /Pied ♂; 25% Normal /Pearl /Pied ♂; 25% Normal /Pied ♀; 25% Pearl /Pied ♀

Normal /Pearl ♂ × Normal /Pied ♀ = 12.5% Normal ♂; 12.5% Normal /Pied ♂; 12.5% Normal /Pearl ♂; 12.5% Normal /Pearl /Pied ♂; 12.5% Normal ♀; 12.5% Normal /Pied ♀; 12.5% Pearl ♀; 12.5% Pearl /Pied ♀

Normal /Pearl ♂ × Pearl /Pied ♀ = 12.5% Pearl ♂; 12.5% Pearl /Pied ♂; 12.5% Normal /Pearl ♂; 12.5% Normal /Pearl /Pied ♂; 12.5% Pearl ♀; 12.5% Pearl /Pied ♀; 12.5% Normal ♀; 12.5% Normal /Pied ♀

Normal /Pearl ♂ × Pied Pearl ♀ = 25% Pearl /Pied ♂; 25% Normal /Pearl /Pied ♂; 25% Pearl /Pied ♀; 25% Normal /Pied ♀

Normal /Pearl /Pied ♂ × Pearl ♀ = 12.5% Pearl ♂; 12.5% Pearl /Pied ♂; 12.5% Normal /Pearl ♂; 12.5% Normal /Pearl /Pied ♂; 12.5% Pearl ♀; 12.5% Pearl /Pied ♀; 12.5% Normal ♀/ 12.5% Normal /Pied ♀

Normal / Pearl /Pied ♂ × Pied ♀ = 12.5% Normal /Pied ♂; 12.5% Pied ♂; 12.5% Normal /Pearl /Pied ♂; 12.5% Pied /Pearl ♂; 12.5% Pearl /Pied ♀; 12.5% Pied Pearl ♀; 12.5% Normal /Pied ♀; 12.5% Pearl ♀

Normal /Pearl /Pied ♂ × Normal /Pied ♀ = 6.25% Normal ♂; 12.5% Normal /Pied ♂; 6.25% Pied ♂; 6.25% Normal /Pearl ♂; 12.5% Normal /Pearl /Pied ♂; 6.25% Pied /Pearl ♂; 6.25% Pearl ♀; 12.5% Pearl /Pied ♀; 6.25% Pied Pearl

♀; 6.25% Normal ♀; 12.5% Normal /Pied ♀; 6.25% Pied ♀

Normal /Pearl /Pied ♂ × Pearl /Pied ♀ = 6.25% Pearl ♂; 12.5% Pearl /Pied ♂; 6.25% Pied Pearl ♂; 6.25% Normal /Pearl ♂; 12.5% Normal /Pearl /Pied ♂; 6.25% Pied /Pearl ♂; 6.25% Pearl ♀; 12.5% Pearl /Pied ♀; 6.25% Pied Pearl ♀; 6.25% Normal ♀; 12.5% Normal /Pied ♀; 6.25% Pied ♀

Normal /Pearl /Pied ♂ × Pied Pearl ♀ = 12.5% Normal /Pearl /Pied ♂; 12.5% Pearl /Pied ♂; 12.5% Pied /Pearl ♂; 12.5% Pied Pearl ♂; 12.5% Normal /Pied ♀; 12.5% Pearl /Pied ♀; 12.5% Pied ♀; 12.5% Pied Pearl ♀

Normal /Pied ♂ × Pearl ♀ = 25% Normal /Pearl ♂; 25% Normal /Pearl /Pied ♂; 25% Normal ♀; 25% Normal /Pied ♀

Normal /Pied ♂ × Pied ♀ = 25% Normal /Pied ♂; 25% Pied ♂; 25% Normal /Pied ♀; 25% Pied ♀

Normal /Pied ♂ × Normal /Pied ♀ = 12.5% Normal ♂; 25% Normal /Pied ♂; 12.5% Pied ♂; 12.5% Normal ♀; 25% Normal /Pied ♀; 12.5% Pied ♀

Normal /Pied ♂ × Pearl /Pied ♀ = 12.5% Normal /Pearl ♂; 25% Normal /Pearl /Pied ♂; 12.5% Pied /Pearl ♂; 12.5% Normal ♀; 25% Normal /Pied ♀; 12.5% Pied ♀

Normal /Pied ♂ × Pied Pearl ♀ = 25% Normal /Pearl /Pied ♂; 25% Pied /Pearl ♂; 25% Normal /Pied ♀; 25% Pied ♀

Pearl /Pied ♂ × Pearl ♀ = 25% Pearl ♂; 25% Pearl /Pied ♂; 25% Pearl ♀; 25% Pearl /Pied ♀

Pearl /Pied ♂ × Pied ♀ = 50% Pied /Pearl ♂; 50% Pied Pearl ♀

Pearl /Pied ♂ × Normal /Pied ♀ = 25% Normal /Pearl /Pied ♂; 25% Pied /Pearl ♂; 25% Pearl /Pied ♀; 25% Pied Pearl ♀

Pearl /Pied ♂ × Pearl /Pied ♀ = 25% Pearl /Pied ♂; 25% Pied Pearl ♂; 25% Pearl /Pied ♀; 25% Pied Pearl ♀

Pearl /Pied ♂ × Pied Pearl ♀ = 25% Pearl /Pied ♂; 25% Pied Pearl ♂; 25% Pearl /Pied ♀; 25% Pied Pearl ♀

Pied Pearl ♂ × Pearl ♀ = 50% Pearl /Pied ♂; 50% Pearl /Pied ♀

Pied Pearl ♂ × Pied ♀ = 50% Pied /Pearl ♂; 50% Pied Pearl ♀

Pied Pearl ♂ × Normal /Pearl ♀ = 25% Normal /Pearl /Pied ♂; 25% Pied /Pearl ♂; 25% Pearl /Pied ♀; 25% Pied Pearl ♀

Pied Pearl ♂ × Pearl /Pied ♀ = 25% Pearl /Pied ♂; 25% Pied Pearl ♂; 25% Pearl /Pied ♀; 25% Pied Pearl ♀

Pied Pearl ♂ × Pied Pearl ♀ = 50% Pied Pearl ♂; 50% Pied Pearl ♀

Table V: Sex-linked Mutations Crossed with Sex-linked Mutations

Though Cinnamon and Pearl were chosen for the example, Lutino may be substituted.

Cinnamon ♂ × Cinnamon ♀ = 50% Cinnamon ♂; 50% Cinnamon ♀

Cinnamon ♂ × Pearl ♀ = 50% Normal /Cinnamon /Pearl ♂; 50% Cinnamon ♀

Pearl ♂ × Cinnamon ♀ = 50% Normal /Pearl /Cinnamon ♂; 50% Pearl ♀

Pearl ♂ × Pearl ♀ = 50% Pearl ♂; 50% Pearl ♀

Normal /Pearl /Cinnamon ♂ × Cinnamon ♀ = 25% Normal /Pearl /Cinnamon ♂; 25% Cinnamon ♂; 25% Pearl ♀; 25% Cinnamon ♀

Normal /Pearl /Cinnamon ♂ × Pearl ♀ = 25% Normal /Pearl /Cinnamon ♂; 25% Pearl ♂; 25% Cinnamon ♀; 25% Pearl ♀

Table VI: Sex-linked Mutations and Crossovers

Step 1 (no crossover):

Lutino ♂ × Pearl ♀ = 50% Normal /Lutino /Pearl ♂; 50% Lutino ♀

Step 2 (50% crossover rate):
Lutino ♂ × Pearl ♀ = 25% Normal /Lutino Pearl ♂; 25% Normal ♂; 50% Lutino ♀

Step 3:
Normal /Lutino /Pearl ♂ × Lutino ♀ = 25% Lutino /Pearl ♂; 25% Normal /Lutino ♂; 25% Lutino Pearl ♀; 25% Normal ♀

The crossover rate is different for different gene characteristics, depending basically on how close or far the gene is located from the center of the chromosome. Experiences by breeders have shown that the crossover rate for Lutino and Pearl is close to 50%, while that for Cinnamon and Pearl may be less.

Table VII: Producing True Albinos

Step 1 pairings:
Whiteface ♂ × Whiteface ♀ = 50% Whiteface ♂; 50% Whiteface ♀

Whiteface ♂ × Lutino ♀ = 50% Normal /Whiteface /Lutino ♂; 50% Normal /Whiteface ♀

Lutino ♂ × Whiteface ♀ = 50% Normal /Lutino /Whiteface ♂; 50% Lutino /Whiteface ♀

Lutino ♂ × Lutino ♀ = 50% Lutino ♂; 50% Lutino ♀

Step 2 (from the possible offspring above, only this pairing will produce Albinos):
Normal /Lutino /Whiteface ♂ × Lutino /Whiteface ♀ = 6.25% Lutino ♂; 6.25% Lutino ♀; 12.5% Lutino /Whiteface ♂; 12.5% Lutino /Whiteface ♀; 6.25% Albino ♂; 6.25% Albino ♀; 6.25% Normal /Lutino ♂; 6.25% Normal ♀; 12.5% Normal /Lutino /Whiteface ♂; 12.5% Normal /Whiteface ♀; 6.25% Whiteface /Lutino ♂; 6.25% Whiteface ♀

BREEDING

Conditioning
If fed a well-balanced diet and allowed to exercise adequately, Cockatiels will come into breeding condition with no additional help from you. While the lengthening of daylight hours triggers the breeding cycle in some species, this is not an important stimulus with Cockatiels. However, for a new breeding pair or for your other birds that have not reached breeding peak when you wished, there are dietary "inducers," assuming that the birds have also been provided with enough space for exercise. Hemp is a stimulating seed. It is expensive, but only a sprinkling is added daily to the diet. Wheat-germ oil is also good and important for fertility. Add a teaspoon to one pound of seed and mix well, but only prepare enough for one or two days' feeding. Do not chance any oil going rancid. Some birds relish the wheat-germ meal itself, which is comparable. Greens should be offered daily and corn (on cob, frozen, or canned) several times a week. Vitamins should be given more frequently, either in the water or as a powdered form sprinkled on corn, greens, or oil-treated seed. Petamine is invaluable, especially for conditioning and as a nestling food.

The vitamins most important in ensuring fertility are B_{12}, E, K, and riboflavin. E and K are found in seed and greens. Riboflavin is also available in green foods. However, birds are most apt to be lacking in B_{12} as it is primarily found in animal protein (in milk, eggs, meat, etc.). One will observe the birds eating their droppings to satisfy this deficiency. Better sources are milk sop (bread moistened with milk) and

Petamine (which contains dried skim milk). Read the labels on your vitamins to be sure that they include B_{12}.

In the wild, birds will not breed until they know that there is a plentiful supply of the proper food to feed their young. Do not hold back on your planned nestling diet, waiting for eggs and hatchlings. The adult birds must be accustomed to the extra foods before they actually embark on parenthood.

Signs of Readiness

If the males and females have been separated prior to breeding, it will become quite obvious when they are ready to breed. The males will be whistling often and heartily, holding their wings out from the body in display. The more aggressive ones will be squabbling with one another. Some will strum the wires of the flights with their beaks. The females will crouch down next to each other on the perch in typical mating stance. All birds will become more active. Not as much time is spent in idle preening or napping. They are alert to any calls from the opposite sex.

If you have kept a pair together, the signs are not as obvious, as absence has not caused the heart to grow fonder. However, if a nest box is in place, their interest will become apparent as they repeatedly go in and out of the box and the male begins to court the hen. If no interest is shown, sometimes simply moving them or the nest box to a new location will be enough of an inducement.

Setting Up

Just before setting the birds up for breeding, one should undertake a thorough cleaning of the breeding cages or flights and nest boxes (the latter should have been cleaned after the previous breeding season). The birds will be working for the next six months approximately and will not appreciate extensive housecleaning, or may not tolerate it at all.

Ideally, the birds and all food and water utensils, mineral blocks, etc., should be removed. New branches should be put up, making certain that they are firmly fixed in place, as an unsteady perch can hamper the birds' balance while mating and result in infertile eggs. Any repairs should be done now, followed by a thorough scrubbing of all walls, wires, and the floor itself. When all has dried, a good dose of mite spray should make your maternity ward safe. Clean floor covering is put down, using more than usual, as droppings will become copious during egg laying and incubation time. Then by removing a bit at a time and replacing it, the birds will not be subjected to a complete change of floor covering. A new cuttlebone, mineral block, and salt spool should be fastened securely. Cleanse seed containers, water bottle, bath dish, and reinstall them. A larger dish than usual should be used for the gravel-and-grit mix, as the birds will be devouring this source of minerals for developing eggs and young. Some breeders add oyster shell to their mixture, but I feel there usually is a sufficient amount already in the mix, and too much can cause shells to be too hard for hatching chicks to pip through.

The Nest Box
The nest box, of course, is very important, as the presence of a suitable nesting site is a necessary stimulus to breeding. Cockatiels are hole, or cavity, breeders, i.e., in the wild they nest in hollow trees or limbs. Breeders dealing with the more difficult species of hole breeders must search the woods to find hollow logs or somehow improvise a natural-looking nest box that will satisfy the birds' demands. Fortunately, Cockatiels are not fussy and will usually accept an enclosure of just about any size or shape that the breeder may provide.

Let me describe in detail the nest box that I have found most practical, and then mention other types. The dimensions are 12" × 12" × 12", with one side consisting of two sliding panels. The top half may be slid open to inspect the eggs or young; the bottom half of the panel remains in place to retain the nesting material, but is removed for cleaning after the clutch has fledged. There are also ventilation holes in the top panel. These provide air circulation when weather is warm. In winter, I cover all but one hole with tape to retain the warmth. The top of the 3″ entrance hole is about 2″ from the top of the box and is positioned off-center. This is desirable because the birds are less apt to jump directly onto their eggs. A dowel is inserted below the entrance, extending about 2 to 3″ into the box as well as on the outside. This interior perch not only facilitates climbing down into and back up out of the box, but the parent birds will find it easier to feed from this level when the babies become large and more crowded. Someone who can wield a hammer and saw with any dexterity should be able to copy this type, or design his own, and include the practical features I have mentioned.

Dimensions are not too important. However, any nest-box floor measuring smaller than 10″ × 10″ can prove detrimental to a large clutch of five or more babies, overcrowded in their final weeks before fledging. Crossed winged tips can be a lasting result, and such birds can never be used for show purposes.

The height of the nest box is least important. The larger parrot species use what is called a very tall, "grandfather clock" box (size varying in proportion to the bird). If you have such a box available (excepting the immense structures made for a macaw or a large cockatoo), it may be suitable for a pair of Cockatiels. Any box measuring more than 15″ from top to bottom should have a ladder inside for the birds to climb. A strip of wire mesh below the hole works well.

Some breeders use a nest box that is longer horizontally than high or wide. For example: 15″ long by 12″ wide by 12″ high. Research uncovered a description of a box 24″ long by 16″ wide by 18″ high, which I would say was rather much, but it illustrates the extremes Cockatiels will accept.

Ready-made boxes will sometimes come with a concave indentation on the bottom, the principle being that the eggs will stay together in one place for incubation, rather than possibly scatter around on the flat surface. This is unnecessary, as it seems better and safer to insulate and cushion the nest-box floor with a "filler." The birds will make their own indentation where they want it, usually in a corner. Sand, rotted wood, bits of paper, oatmeal, wheat bran, grass clippings, processed corn cob, or cut-up hay may be used as nesting material. I prefer Litter Green (a commercial product used for cat pans) mixed with some wood chips and cedar shavings (which will discourage mites). More material may be added as the chicks grow and the droppings build up.

Many novices put out cotton, bits of string bits, etc., thinking that Cockatiels actually build nests like a canary. No! In the wild, they might chew the wooden interior of their enclosure to enlarge the space. The only nesting material would be the resulting scraps and pieces that fall to the bottom of the hollow.

Placement of the Nest Box
If your birds are to breed in a cage, it is far better to attach the nest box to the outside of the cage, so as not to take up any needed space within the already small enclosure. Even in flight cages, I prefer to attach the box to the outside of the wire so that I can check eggs or young easily, without upsetting the parents even further by entering their inner sanctum.

The birds seem to prefer the boxes being placed up high; however, do not situate them where the noonday sun will hit the entrance hole and thus cause overheating of the nest and its inhabitants.

If a pair that is presumably in breeding condition do not accept a nest box in a particular location after two weeks, it may be that they do not like the location, or possibly not the nest box itself. Try moving the box to a new location or setting up a different sized box. In a colony flight, keep the nest boxes as far away from each other as possible, so there will be less arguing over territories.

For future reference, know which pair preferred which type of nest box and placement. If the birds were fussy one year, it may save time the next breeding season to accommodate them with the setup previously proven.

Make sure that the nest boxes are attached securely to the wire or the walls. Use at least three screw hooks for hanging the box. If one hook should come out, the other two should still hold. I lost one clutch of chicks when the nest box came loose, fell to the cement floor, and cracked open. In the morning, I found the parents diligently feeding the chicks scattered about the floor. There was no apparent physical harm from the fall itself, but the unfeathered babies soon died from chilling. A disaster such as this hurts, as it was through no fault of the birds and was unnecessary.

Record Keeping

When breeding birds, especially more than one pair, it is best not to rely on memory alone. Banding the birds makes each an individual by means of a number, but records must be kept if the numbers are to mean anything.

I attach an index card to each nest box. A member of our local club makes convenient metal holders for these cards to slip into, but even a tack or piece of tape is sufficient. I put the names of the hen and male at the top, followed by any information pertinent to setting them up. Then I make two columns entitled Laid and Hatched. The number between the two denotes the number of days the eggs took to hatch. (This is not really a necessary notation, just curiosity and research on my part.) Band numbers are noted to the right of the hatching column, and also if the bird is a male or female (supposing they are the result of a cross that means that they can be sexed in the nest). I draw a line through the date for any chicks that die, or indicate whether an unhatched egg was infertile, punctured, dead in shell, etc. Each clutch is given a new card. These cards can then be filed away for reference.

I also keep duplicate entries in a "little black book" (or one might use a file box) on a writing desk near the telephone. This is more practical than running back and forth to the birds. As a bird is sold or traded, I circle the band number, note the buyer's or trader's name and address, and the date of sale. Apart from the young birds, I also keep a separate section for breeders, pets, etc. (in other words, my "permanent" birds), noting from whom I bought each and when, or from which of my own pairs he or she was hatched and the hatching date. Also I note with which bird(s) he or she has been paired, preferred food, whether aggressive when breeding, and awards won—anything furthering that bird's individuality.

It is difficult to keep referring to a bird as 4R-75 or 37-83, etc., so I find it easier to name every permanent bird, whether or not he or she is a pet. They end up with some pretty dumb titles, but they don't care and I can tell more quickly who is Dead-eye Dick (he's blind in one eye), Flecks (she has a few white feathers on her neck), Her (obviously a hen), or Lothrop (named after the man I bought him from), and Mama and Papa (my original pair).

You may not want to get as detailed, but keeping some sort of records is a must. You will definitely need them when choosing suitable pairs for breeding or to determine which bird is split and to which mutation, to distinguish adult Pearl males who have lost their spots from Normal males, etc.

Mating and Eggs

It all seems so simple when you can say, "Okay, today all is ready, and we shall begin the breeding season!" You place male with female in appropriately prepared cage, and voilà, the birds mate within minutes. (Things are more complicated when the birds are together for weeks and couldn't care less—this means you need to pay more attention to conditioning them.)

All systems are go when the male whistles, flies about, pursues the female on the perch with wings held out from the body, bowing, and nodding—perhaps he or both of them chatter their beaks. A moment or two may be spent inspecting the nest box. Now he may strum a tune for her with his beak on the wires of the flight. Finally, the hen indicates that she is adequately impressed and will crouch down on the perch, back horizontal, tail elevated, crest lowered, and the male will mount her. He will chatter his beak, emitting a repetitive chirping sound as he gyrates his tail to the side and finally copulates by working his vent into position under her tail. Very good balance is needed, and one can see why an unsteady perch would be detrimental! The mating act itself can take as long as a full minute. He then flies off, and she commences to preen herself.

They will mate repeatedly for many days. The first egg will be laid any time from one to two weeks after the initial mating. As the time draws near for her first egg, she will spend more time in the nest box and seem to gorge herself on cuttlebone, mineral block, and the gravel-grit mix. She is making an eggshell. About 24 hours before she is to drop her egg, her ventral area may appear swollen and her lower back slightly humped. A few large, copious droppings will be seen on the floor. (The parents are "toilet trained" in the nest box, and therefore will store up, so to speak, and eliminate less often but with bigger results when they do leave the nest box).

If a hen has never laid before, do not be alarmed if the first egg has a smear of blood on it or if it is more elongated. I was surprised to find that a chick could actually develop normally and hatch from such a misshaped egg!

Cockatiel eggs are white, average 6.5 grams in weight, and are laid on alternate days, although occasionally you will find eggs laid one day apart. The average clutch is four to six eggs. I have had as many as eight babies in one nest, and there are records of even more being laid, hatched, and raised successfully. Jim Jankowski of Chicago had a hen lay 15 fertile eggs. All hatched and survived, although some were fostered out, some hand-fed, and the remainder raised by the parents.

The male sperm is long lived. I have not come across actual statistics about this, but the following is an illustration from my own experience. A particular pair was raising a clutch of babies that I did not feel were top quality, and I did not want a second clutch. Therefore when I saw the pair mating again while the first youngsters were still in the nest, I decided I would separate the pair. The male was left in the flight to feed and wean the young, and the hen was removed to another cage with a nest box so she could lay her eggs, which I assumed would by then be infertile. She laid a total of six eggs, the first three proving fertile though they were laid ten to fourteen days after mating!

Canary breeders replace newly laid eggs with dummies or infertile eggs collected from past nests. (The "stolen" eggs are kept safe and turned twice daily, end over end.) The breeder then replaces all the real eggs when the hen has completed her egg laying, the principal reason being that the eggs will then hatch simultaneously and all the chicks will be equal in size and age. Otherwise, the older chicks, being larger, can crowd out their younger siblings at feeding time. This practice is not a must with Cockatiels, as all the young seem to be fed fairly, not just the nearest and biggest mouths. This seems amazing, as in a clutch of six, seven, or even eight young, the oldest chick may be more than two weeks of age (feathering in and approximately ten times larger than a hatchling); nonetheless, good parents still find those tiniest of mouths to feed.

EGG BINDING. While hens are laying their clutches, egg binding is the main concern. It can be caused by lack of exercise, a hen that has not matured sufficiently, cold temperatures, deficiency in diet, or a combination of any of these. I was worried the first year when I bred my birds in the winter and temperatures in the bird room averaged around 55° F. However, this apparently was not too cold, as I have never had a case of egg binding. (Knock on wood, or tomorrow I'll find three hens in distress.)

The warning signs are a hen puffed up on the perch, or worse yet, on the floor of the cage or flight, perhaps with her head tucked in her feathers. She may strain occasionally in an effort to pass the egg. Prolonged straining will exhaust the hen. Some birds will expel the egg in good time and be none the worse for wear; however, others must have help. Heat will relax the affected muscles. A heating pad, hospital cage, or any source of heat is good. Even holding the bird over steam may do the trick, if the bird is not unduly upset by the handling. Spread your fingers so that the vent is exposed, and pay attention to the amount of heat on your hand—if it is too hot for your fingers, it is too hot for the bird. Sometimes injecting a bit of olive oil into the vent will sufficiently ease the passage of the egg, but be very careful that you do not puncture the egg itself. Usually any hen that has been egg bound should be rested for three months.

SOFT-SHELLED EGG. A soft-shelled egg sometimes occurs. This is an egg that may be laid with no shell at all(just a membrane holding the yolk and albumen) or with a very soft, pliable covering, probably misshapen. This is usually attributed to a lack of either minerals or the capacity to properly assimilate the minerals. My beloved pet, the original Jelly Bean, died of a soft-shelled egg that ruptured internally. I cannot believe her diet was wanting, as she was the best and most varied eater of all my flock, sampling any goodie I offered. She had laid two normal eggs and then appeared to be having trouble with her third. Rather than catch her up and disturb her further, as she did not seem overly distressed, I left her in her flight. Finally, by late afternoon I found her happily sitting on her first eggs in the nest box. Scratching her head, I said good night. I then spotted a broken soft-shelled egg on the floor under a perch. I assumed it had broken in its fall to the floor and felt all was again fine. However, in the morning I found Jelly Bean dead in the box, still faithfully atop her first two eggs. I could not do a postmortem myself nor did I want anyone else to touch a scalpel to her. Silly, I suppose, in the light of possibly furthering scientific knowledge, but she was a member of our family and her death touched us all so deeply. Anyway, I felt it was possible that the egg had broken internally, allowing passage of the egg and relief to her, but ultimately this led to peritonitis as a result of some of the egg remaining internally. Her first two eggs I fostered out; they proved fertile but died within a week of hatching. How I wanted her son or daughter!

Breeders of any species of birds will agree that it seems that we always lose our best bird. I swear, if I hatch the first *plaid* Cockatiel, it will promptly keel over before I can even detect its clan affiliation (although more problems and mortalities would be expected in the development of a new mutation). It's not that we lose only our best, but I guess we quickly forget the others as their passing does not touch us as seriously or for so long.

Incubation

The parent bird sitting in the nest with his or her breast in contact with the eggs, thus providing the required heat for each embryo to develop, is called incubation. In performing this feat, the parents are seeking their own comfort. Their breast temperature is greatly increased, and the eggs serve to cool it; therefore, their turning of the eggs is actually the realization by the bird that the other side of the shell will be cooler and more soothing. Thus the parent bird is made comfortable, and the chick develops by being warmed from every side—a mutually agreeable arrangement.

Serious incubation usually starts after the second or third egg has been laid, the male sitting by day and the hen at night. Often the pair will sit together in the nest box, sharing the eggs beneath them (during hatching, babies may be under one, eggs under the other). Usually, as more eggs are laid, the steadier the birds become when you check the nest box. But remember, by being nosy, you do chance panicking the birds, which might result in broken or punctured eggs or, worse yet, total desertion of the nest. Know your pairs and how much interference they will tolerate.

Should an egg be punctured or slightly cracked, all is not lost. The danger here to the developing chick is the chance of dehydration (evaporation of the albumen) or, when it is more fully developed, the membrane may adhere to its body. One can use the egg white from a chicken egg, coating the puncture or crack with it. Let it dry and then place the egg back in the nest, being sure that nothing adheres to this "glue" as it dries. Mrs. Moon saved infertile eggs using bits of the shells to patch good eggs. A tiny touch of clear nail polish can be used as a glue or just to cover a tiny hole; or even a bit of cellophane tape may suffice.

Fertility

Once eggs are laid, the next question is whether they are fertile. With a bit of experience, one can tell at a glance once the eggs are ten to fourteen days old. Well-developed eggs will appear a flat white; infertile or newly laid eggs will look translucent: yellow-pinkish, not solid.

One can hold an egg up to a ray of sunlight or over a flashlight to see if the egg has started to "vein" at about a week of age. Or you can go to further lengths by cutting a hole in a piece of cardboard (smaller than the egg, so that the egg can set into the aperture), then holding the board directly over a light. This is called "candling" (in the old days, with poultry eggs, a candle's flame was used for the light source). This method is good, as the board shields the eye from the light, all of which is directed through the egg. At about five days of age, the interior of a fertile egg should show a network of red blood vessels forming. When older, the developing chick's body becomes more obvious as a dark mass.

Remember, you are handling a delicate and hopefully precious cargo. While man may have a long way to go in inventing as perfect and functional a packaging design as the eggshell, it is by necessity fragile. Holding the egg by the two ends is safer than grasping by pinching the sides.

Should you end up with infertile eggs, save a few. They are interesting for "show and tell." People are interested in seeing and surprised at the size of a Cockatiel's egg. Also, as previously noted, bits of shell may come in handy for patching good eggs.

Chilling

Do not despair if the eggs are not constantly incubated by one or the other of the parents. Apparently the eggs can often survive and will develop, despite prolonged lapses in attention by the parent birds, especially at the beginning and end of the development period. Chilling is of most concern at midterm.

I read of a person in England whose Cockies stayed off the eggs for two entire nights and were on and off the eggs during the day. When the decision to remove the eggs was finally made, he discovered they had hatched! Alice L. Sadler tells of her experience when heating problems necessitated moving a cage with six eggs. As a result, the parents came off the eggs at 10:00 A.M. and did not go back to incubate until 6:00 P.M. Meanwhile, the room temperature was in the low sixties, yet all the eggs hatched eventually. These illustrations are exceptions, and the developing chicks must have been very strong, as weaker individuals would have been more likely to succumb under such circumstances.

Bathing and Other Notes

While the parent birds incubate their eggs, a water dish is a must. At other times of the year Cockatiels may ignore such a receptacle, but they do seem to appreciate the opportunity for a good soaking when breeding. The bath not only cools and refreshes the adults but, upon returning to the eggs, the moisture from their wet feathers increases the humidity in the nest box. If hatching is imminent, this aids the chick by softening the eggshell. A water spraying is also advised to raise the ambient humidity, and whichever parent is "off duty" may appreciate the shower too.

If eggs are to be fostered out, you must mark each egg with a dot, an *X*, or some symbol so that you will know for your records which pair are the natural parents and thus be certain of the chick's inheritance. Mercurochrome is good for marking not only the eggs but also any chicks that are switched to a foster nest. The chick that hatches from a marked egg must then be immediately marked so that, when old enough to be properly banded, its records will accurately reflect its real ancestry. Be sure that the mark does not wear off; reapply as the stain fades.

I have noticed that during incubation and when chicks begin to hatch there is a strong acrid smell to the normally odorless droppings of the adult birds. This seems to be a normal part of the cycle, and the birds have not shown any signs of distress or illness. I simply put down a surplus of floor-covering material or extra sheets of newspaper that can be removed quickly and more often.

Hatching

As hatching commences and continues, one or both of the parent birds are usually in constant attendance. If the adult is steady enough to nudge aside, you will be able to see the tiny, newborn chick. The body is usually covered with yellow fuzz in Normals and most mutations. The exceptions are the Whiteface and Albino mutations, where the chick lacks all lipochrome and will have totally white down on the body.

Some mutations can be identified at birth (before feathers appear): the Lutino, Fallow, and Albino. Their eyeballs, behind the closed lids, are pink bulges; any Normals and other mutations will be dark.

If the parents will not allow an actual "sighting," a quick check of the nest box will show the two halved shells as proof of a hatching.

The young chick is equipped with an "egg tooth": a hard, pointed white "knob" near the tip of its upper mandible. As it maneuvers itself around within the egg, it chips away at the confining shell with this tooth, making a complete circle and finally cracking the encasement in half. A babe is born! The egg tooth wears off or grows out as the beak develops, and by three weeks of age is barely noticeable at the tip of the beak.

During hatching, the final remains of the egg yolk (attached to the abdomen) are absorbed into the body, supplying energy for the task of hatching and nourishment for the hours following. While attentive parents will usually start feeding the chick before it is twelve hours old, it can usually survive on its own for this initial period.

Due Date

One can expect hatching anywhere between 18 to 21 days after each egg was laid. Thus each egg hatches in sequence, usually two days apart, although sometimes you will be surprised to find two newborns on the same day . Usually the first egg or two will hatch closer to 21 days, as the parent birds may not have commenced serious incubation until after the second or even third egg was laid.

Don't remove eggs too soon, thinking they are dead! Allow at least 28 days. Perhaps the first eggs died in developing, but the later eggs may still be good. I find the parents will incubate about four weeks maximum, and then lose interest, either knowing all is lost or tiring from the effort.

Any obviously fertile eggs that have failed to hatch should be opened so that you gain some insight into the cause. Again, do not open before 28 days! It is heartbreaking to crack a shell only to find a live chick close to full term. It will of course die. Usually though, you will find the embryo dead at an earlier stage of development. This could be a result of chilling or an inherent weakness in the chick.

It is not unusual that one or maybe two eggs fail to hatch. Remember that nature allows for the possibility of failures, and many eggs are laid. In the wild, perhaps only a very few of these eggs hatch and young survive to be successfully weaned. Even under the aviculturist's controlled conditions, one should not feel badly when results aren't one hundred percent. However, with a subnormal hatching of just two or three eggs, you should suspect that something is wrong (perhaps the breeders are too old, not in top condition, too closely related, too young; the shells too hard; the humidity too low, etc.).

Humidity

Humidity can be an important factor at hatching time. Remember that the shell is porous, allowing for the exchange of oxygen and carbon dioxide as the embryo develops. If conditions are too dry during incubation (or the egg is punctured), moisture will evaporate from the egg. Sometimes you will find an egg that "rattles" when shook. This egg has been completely dehydrated, the contents drying into a hard kernel.

Some shells may be harder than others, and additional moisture will ease the chick's struggle to crack the shell. During hot weather, additional moisture may become a real necessity. In summer, spray the parent birds with water, as well as the cages (avoiding the food dishes); even sparingly spray the eggs and nest-box interior as hatching time approaches. If some chicks have already hatched, don't spray them, but wet the remaining eggs with a wet finger.

However, if the parents have been given a bathing dish, they will provide their eggs with the moisture from their breast feathers. If the room humidity has not been unduly depleted by heat (under 50%), the eggs will hatch with no further assistance from you. I find 60–70% humidity is best.

While I am belaboring the humidity bit (and this is not usually as big a problem as I have now managed to make it sound), a friend of mine read of a simple solution to his hatching problems. He was having horrendous troubles hatching his Australian parakeets in his warm and therefore dry cellar. Nest after nest were full term but dead in the shell, despite sprayings of the flights and water dishes available to the parent birds. Somewhere he read about mixing a generous handful of salt with the nesting material, so that the salt would absorb any available moisture and raise the humidity in the nest box. Bingo! He has had no further problems. This might be just the solution for someone else who has been repeatedly disappointed.

Helping a Chick to Hatch

I have tried to help many chicks to hatch if there appears to be a problem, but I recall a low percentage surviving to adulthood. (Some might survive two weeks or more and then succumb.) Despite obstacles of perhaps too hard or too dry a shell, a truly strong chick can usually crack the shell itself. Although a sometimes exhausting experience, the throes of hatching are a part of the initial test in the survival of the fittest.

It takes a chick approximately 36 to 48 hours to hatch. Its birth begins by its inflicting tiny fractures around the mid-section of the eggshell as it rotates within. Its head is encased in the larger, more rounded end of the egg. You can hear its tiny chirps if you listen carefully as you inspect the egg. Some chicks will make a large opening in the shell at a single spot. This can be bad, as moisture may evaporate too quickly and the membrane just beneath the shell may dry out, adhering to the chick's body and not allowing it to turn and crack the remaining circumference. If you observe such a hole and the chick is overdue in hatching, you might place a smear of warm water on the hole (to remoisten the membrane), being super careful not to drown the chick, as its nostrils and mouth will be right at the opening. In general this is a rather risky procedure.

Sometimes a chick will have pipped part way around the egg, but has been exhausted by perhaps an abnormally hard shell and nothing further happens. When hatching is overdue, in this instance too (as with the dried membrane above), you can very carefully pry the egg open. This is a last resort, before the chick is poisoned within the shell by its own excrement as its kidneys and bowels begin to function externally. Do not be disappointed, as the odds are usually low for survival; probably the chick was a weakling to begin with—but you tried.

Timing is so very critical! Sometimes you are sure the chick is overdue in hatching, only to find in opening the shell that the egg yolk is still in evidence on the abdomen,

Pearl nestlings, about three weeks old. Photo by Horst Bielfeld.

and the chick actually needed 12 to 24 hours more time. Give yourself 42 kicks! I hate to think of how many chicks I may actually have murdered because of overconcern and eagerness. The few lucky guesses I have made when a chick was truly full term and in trouble are in the minority. I hesitate even to mention this subject. However, there are a few times when you do end up the hero. But otherwise, know that you are not alone with your terrible guilt feelings when you've misjudged.

The First Twenty-four Hours

The first 24 hours after hatching are the most critical; the mortality rate decreases with each additional day. Many that do die might have been dead-in-shell statistics, but somehow they managed to hatch, too weak to wiggle and beg for food, dying belatedly.

The last one or two chicks in a large nest of six or more young may fare better if fostered out to a smaller clutch with chicks of more similar age and size. Its older siblings might prove too much for such a tiny chick. In order to keep track of the fostered baby from his new nest mates, mark him with mercurochrome. The stain must be renewed often, until the chick is old enough to be banded and identification can be made permanent.

If a fostered nest of similar-aged chicks is not available, do not despair, as a strong chick can, despite the odds, usually survive and eventually catch up in size to its initially monstrous siblings. In many species of birds, this would not be the case.

Any egg that fails to hatch should be left in the nest for at least a week, as it serves as a support to the hatchlings much as a sibling's body does. Should a parent sit too tightly on her young, the egg will prevent her squashing the smallest baby. When the young become larger than the egg, the egg may be removed and finally opened to determine the cause of its not hatching.

If the egg's contents appear "clear" (only yolk and albumen), it was infertile. If there is evidence of veins or even a tiny embryo (the eye being the most prominent feature), the chick most likely died from chilling or an inherent weakness during the early stages of development. An addled egg contains a brownish mass: a decomposed embryo. (Not all dead eggs spoil.) If the egg holds the recognizable form of a developed chick, it obviously died close to full term. Again this could be from chilling or weakness, or, if fully developed, the shell could have proven too thick or too dry to crack. A partially pipped egg indicates that the chick became too weak and was slow in completing its chore. The membrane adhered to its body and prevented it from further rotation (suspect low humidity).

Feeding

While your birds incubate their eggs, plan well ahead and make sure you will have plenty of seed and other items in plentiful supply. Anticipate someone totaling the family car, the blizzard of the century, the seed factory burning down; in other words, be prepared. And talk about raising teenaged children! Cockatiel chicks, in proportion to body size, can shame any class at the local high school when it comes to food intake.

I find that the resulting size of a young bird depends far more on the parents' job in feeding and the quantity, as well as the nutritional quality of the food made available to the pair, than on inheritance. This does not mean that one should completely ignore the genetic factors, and purchase an emaciated pair of birds for breeding–always start with the best stock that you can afford and aim for the babies to surpass their parents. If you can only feed your birds once a day, put out extra dishes. Do not make them spend valuable time and energy searching through husks for good seed. Each chick's food intake will grow as it grows, climaxing at around three weeks of age, then tapering off a bit as it slims down in preparation for fledging.

Above: A *triple* cross-mutation—a Cinnamon Pearl Pied hen in a flight with Blue-winged Grass-Parakeets. Photo by Dale R. Thompson and George D. Dodge. **Facing page:** A Cinnamon male with a Cinnamon Pearl female. Photo by Horst Bielfeld.

Cockatiels feed their young by first filling their own crop with husked seed and whatever other delicacies you have chosen to offer. Each parent returns to the nest and regurgitates this mixture into each tiny, begging mouth by pumping the neck up and down while hooking bills with the youngster. Budgerigars will lay each baby on its back to feed, but the Cockatiel chick will stand up and stretch its neck to the parent. (Therefore, Budgies usually cannot be considered as emergency foster parents for very young Cockies—lovebirds might be a better bet but they may be dubious about their strange foster child.)

You will hear the characteristic peep-peep-peep of a chick as it is being fed; and as it grows, so does its voice. If you have a very shy pair of birds, hearing this feeding song is better than chancing a peek. The sound is proof enough that a chick is there and being attended.

Because the parents must regurgitate freely and often, the birds will drink more water and prefer softer foods such as corn, milk-sop, Petamine, or powdered nestling food to make the process easier, especially when the chicks are under one week of age. Be sure that the pair always has a plentiful supply of fresh water.

A rabbit salt spool (or iodized table salt in a small dish) is relished and, in fact, seemingly demanded when feeding young. This is not a unique characteristic, but has been observed in many species of birds, most especially by psittacines that frequent salt licks in the wild. However, if you are giving your birds granulated salt for the first time, offer a very small amount, so that they don't overdo at the beginning. Salt spools, being hard, are safer, as the bird has to really work to get an appreciable amount.

Charcoal granules, if you do not normally use them in your gravel-grit mix, seem to be especially appreciated at this time. It is a good precaution against sour crop, as the charcoal sweetens the stomach. Approximately one tablespoon to a cup of gravel-grit mix is sufficient. In recent years charcoal, gravel, and grit have been eliminated from many bird diets.

Nestling Foods and Other Nourishment

Marie Olssen recommended bread crumbs mixed with mashed hard-boiled egg and grated carrot. Many people will make a milk-sop, using a nutritious bread (whole or cracked wheat, etc.) moistened with milk. Shredded-wheat biscuits treated similarly have also been suggested.

Just be sure that any food containing milk or eggs does not sour, especially during hot weather. If you are away from home for the whole day, it might be safer to use water as the moistener.

For some reason, my birds have yet to take to any of the above nourishing recipes. However, Petamine alone, or a comparable nestling or conditioning mix, is as good, if not better, being more completely balanced nutritionally, and it will not sour. Outside the breeding season, my birds will eat only a small bit of Petamine daily, but when chicks begin to hatch, it is devoured. As the babies reach about two weeks of age, most parents then seem to become obsessed with sunflower seed and consume a lesser amount of the parakeet or Cockatiel mix, but still eating a large amount of Petamine.

The food item that I have found to be perhaps the biggest bonus in encouraging and enabling parent birds to feed and raise robust young is corn, sprinkled with my "special" mix and served twice daily. I prefer raw corn on the cob, but canned or frozen kernels are fine (especially when ears cost thirty cents apiece during the winter months, or are not available at any price). The birds seem to relish this delicacy any time of year, but when feeding young, they become fanatics! Even my shyest birds will stand within inches of my hand as I replenish their portion. I cut raw ears lengthwise, resulting in two flat-sided pieces, which are more stable than a whole cob that rolls when the parents are trying to eat. I then cut off the very tops of the kernels, exposing the interior for easy extraction (they do not eat the kernel's casing). I feed these trimmings too, as they will clean out the meat from each kernel. My friends laugh at the time I take in preparing my cobs. Perhaps I should only do this cutting rou-

Above: A newly hatched chick with three older, Normal siblings. Even with such a difference in size, a strong chick can compete and survive. Photo by Jerry Kessler.

Facing page: A Young Pied male, attractively marked. It is unusual for a Pied bird carrying this much gray not to have a "dirty face" (gray feathers mixed into the white-and-yellow head area, and a fault on the show bench). Photo by Horst Bielfeld.

tine at the start to get the birds to discover the delicacy, but I feel that whatever steps I can take to save the parents' time spent in obtaining food (and that also means not having to hunt for some uneaten kernel at the bottom of a dish), the more often the babies are fed, the faster they grow, and the less energy is drained from the hard-working parents. (No, I have not as yet started to husk sunflower!)

My "Reed's Mix" is kept in jar that has holes in the top for dispensing—but whatever the container, it must have a tight lid to keep moisture out. The mix consists of equal parts of powdered vitamins (I use Necton), plain, unflavored gelatin, and iodized salt. This is thoroughly mixed and sprinkled on the freshly cut corncobs (or the canned or frozen kernels). If you use corncobs and do not cut them, wet the ears so that the mixture will adhere.

The salt and vitamins have been mentioned before, but let's discuss the purpose of the gelatin. This is made from the skin and bones of animals and is therefore a source of protein, which is a necessary nutrient for growth and not usually found in sufficient quantity in seed alone. The package will usually state that gelatin is not a significant source of protein, but this is referring more to human needs. Another plus for the babies is that it is easily digested.

Greens are also usually relished during this period, chickweed being probably the most favored of all. Most abundant in spring and to a lesser degree in summer and fall, you can dig up clumps of it, wash well, serve to the birds, and within hours the plant will have been reduced to a stump. When chickweed is not available, other greens must be offered—the greener the leaf, the more nutritious it will be. Head lettuce is next to useless, but romaine and chicory are good; collards, beets, mustard, and dandelion greens, kale, watercress, parsley, etc., are better. Usually you will have to stick with the ones the birds have been accustomed to. With the exception of chickweed, I find they do not quickly accept a different "salad."

Millet sprays are another food that is usually liked. These can be offered dry or soaked to the point that the seeds begin to germinate (when the white tips begin to appear), which heightens the nutritional value. Parakeet mix may also be treated in this manner. Soak millet sprays (or seed mix) in a sieve set in a container of water, changing the water twice daily so it will not become sour. One can rinse well after twenty-four hours and serve, or soak longer, until shoots are just breaking through the husks.

Following is a listing of possible foods and supplements while young are being raised. One can of course add or substitute items, the point being that, for success, the greater the variety and sources of good nutrition offered, the more likely the parents will become good feeders and raise young you will be proud of. Allow more time for preparation and feeding, and be generous, especially with seed. Sunflower seed; parakeet or Cockatiel mix; Petamine or a nestling or conditioning mix; gravel-grit-charcoal mix; cuttlebone and mineral block (some birds may prefer one more than the other); fresh water; greens; millet spray (dry or soaked), corn with vitamin-gelatin-salt mix; salt spools; milk-sop (optional).

Growing and Weaning

The first seven weeks for a young Cockatiel are the most critical of its life, and the most draining on the parents. Laying eggs and incubation require very little energy for the adult birds, but feeding a good-sized clutch of chicks will take its toll on parents unless they are in top condition. Do as much for them as possible, and in return they will reward you with their efforts.

FIRST TWO WEEKS. As the chicks hatch, they will huddle together for warmth and support by entwining their necks over and around each other's shoulders, keeping their tiny, round bottoms to the outside of the circle. Sometimes it becomes hard to count noses, and you must separate the mass into individuals in order to account for each.

Above: A Lutino mother Cockatiel and two chicks, with a third just hatched. Photo by Jerry Kessler.

Facing page: Young Pied Cockatiel with feathers trimmed for taming. Photo by Isabelle Francais.

The rate of growth in these first two weeks is astounding! One can actually, at a glance, tell which chick has hatched in what sequence—two days can make a big difference!

Between eight and fourteen days of age, the chicks will be large enough to band, the eyes will open, and the feather sheaths will begin to emerge, the wing flights and crest feathers first. By this stage, the parents will begin to stay out of the nest box for longer periods of time, the young being able to generate enough body heat from the mass of their bodies combined, despite their lack of a feather covering. The crop will be consistently bulging, almost equaling the size of the bird's abdomen. It is hard to believe that such a naked, clumsy, disproportioned "ugly duckling" could ever develop into the beautiful and graceful proportions of an adult bird.

Toward the two-week mark, you may check the babies in the late afternoon and all is well, only to find a chick dead in the morning. (I like to check my babies twice a day, so that should any problem arise, it is discovered soon enough to take appropriate measures, as such a young bird can die very quickly.) Although this "two-week death syndrome" is not a common occurrence, it just seems to happen often enough to mention. Cause?—I have yet to discover it. Postmortems have not been conclusive, but I hope to be able to research this further. Perhaps there is a transitional phase at this age that for some proves fatal.

And while we are being pessimistic, let's mention other possible problems that may crop up. Sometimes a young chick may somehow become separated from the group and become chilled. Often he will appear to be dead, but if not too much time has elapsed, there is hope that he can be revived by warming him in your hands and breathing on him, or by utilizing some other quick source of heat. Or maybe a chick seems weak and his crop is empty, having perhaps missed a feeding, so that now he does not have the energy to beg for his supper. A supplemental feeding from you may be all that is needed. Should your efforts fail, realize that there may have been a legitimate reason that the bird got into such a situation—an inherent weakness that must prove fatal according to nature's law.

THREE TO FOUR WEEKS. At around three weeks of age, the chicks will look like a cross between a turtle and a porcupine. Each baby's head and beak resembles a turtle's, while the body covered with needle-like feather sheaths suggests that a porcupine was its parent. And what a crop! A young Cockie, after a good feed, looks like a pillow tied in the middle—the top half all food.

It is also interesting at this stage to note the linear pattern that the feathers make as they emerge. One would think that an adult bird was feathered all over, but no! Note how much open space there is between the rows of feather follicles themselves. As the feathers burst their sheaths and fan out, to be further insulated by each feather's supplement of down, the bird appears to be covered, yet the "roots" themselves are relatively few and far between.

It is at this feathering-out stage that one can get the first idea of the quality of the young. How bald are the Lutinos, how heavy are the Pieds, how pearled the Pearls?—or whatever colorations you were seeking. If you used a cross where the young can be sexed in the nest, the females and split males become obvious also. This is a fun time.

By now the nest box may be getting a bit ripe. Although the droppings can prove a source of heat in themselves, if there is an unpleasant odor or too much moisture, so that each dropping does not dry into a pellet, it is best to add more nesting material or, if really necessary, clean out and replace it completely. If the chicks have not feathered out, and your material has been stored in a cold area, it might be best to warm it a bit before placing it in the box to prevent the chicks from being chilled. Remember that normal droppings in themselves are not "dirty"; note how the chicks' plumage is usually very clean. Realize that in the wild, your housekeeping would not be available.

Above: Two of the three nestlings are Pearls, evidenced by yellow quills on the shoulders. The third chick is a Normal. Photo by Nancy A. Reed. **Below:** A Pearl chick about two weeks old. Photo by Michael Gilroy.

Above: A Pearl chick, about four weeks old. Photo by Horst Bielfeld. **Below:** A Lutino chick and a Pearl chick. Photo by W. Loeding.

Also, at this point one should be handling the babies, taking each in turn from the nest box and holding, playing, and rubbing the backs of each neck for a few moments. Thus each will become accustomed to the human presence that it will experience for the rest of its life, whether it becomes a pet, a show bird, or a breeder. Caution must be used so that the bird does not jump unexpectedly from your hand and fall to the floor (usually fatal); or, if placed on a flat surface, that it does not back off an edge in the typical crawfish-like manner of a baby Cockatiel. It is also great at grasping everything with those eight little claws. Do not be impatient and pull the bird loose by force, as you may sprain the chick's foot or cause a more permanent injury. The purpose is to promote confidence in the bird, not to inflict injury or instill further fear by rough handling.

PLUCKING AND HUNGER LINES. As the feathers emerge, you may discover that the babies are being plucked by a parent, most likely the hen. The area involved is usually the head, neck, and back, while the flight feathers are allowed to grow. This is a very frustrating problem, but fortunately not usually serious, as the baby will regrow these feathers quickly when weaned. However, should the plucking become more like biting, resulting in serious bleeding, the delinquent parent must be removed, leaving the other to feed and raise the young (or you must resort to hand-feeding).

The cause of plucking is conjectural: lack of something in the diet, a desire to nest again, overaffection, or maybe just plain boredom while sitting in the nest box. It is not always a consistent practice either. Perhaps a parent will pluck only the first clutch in some years, or only after the babies have left the nest (often in this latter case the male becomes impatient, wanting to be done with the responsibility of the present clutch, anxious to get on to another.)

While babies are still in the nest, it may help somewhat to put oatmeal flakes, tiny twigs, or millet sprays into the nest box for the parent to chew on instead of the young. I have asked many breeders for other suggestions. One was to mix a capsule of powdered quinine with a 1¾ oz. jar of petroleum jelly and apply this to the plucked area. I have tried this repeatedly in desperation, but it did not seem to make any difference, other than the parents' feathers became filthy as a result. Listerine mixed 1:1 with water was also tried, but with no better results. Someone suggested alum, but after purchasing it, I noted that the label stated that it was harmful if taken internally, so I never took the chance. If someone has a sure cure, we would all like to hear it!

However, as the problem is more temporarily unsightly than debilitating permanently, and not apparently hereditary but more circumstantial, I grumble a few obscenities at the parents and resign myself to waiting a few more weeks to finally see what beauty God hath wrought.

"Hunger lines" signify a diet deficiency or interruption in the chick's feeding. They are obvious on close inspection as a line or lines running across the feather, perpendicular to the shaft. Especially noticeable on the longer wing and tail flights, they weaken the feather, and it may break off. Amino acids are needed for feather growth. These cannot be stored in the body, so the supply must be constant and sufficient. When lacking, the visible sign becomes obvious as each feather is "starved" and in effect stunted momentarily, forming such lines. Unflavored gelatin, Petamine or a similar mixture, or milk sop should eliminate the likelihood or correct any further occurrence of hunger lines.

FOUR TO FIVE WEEKS. The time has come to leave the nest; the feathers now cover the body and the tail flights. Although the feathers are not fully grown, they are sufficient to enable the chick to fly. As the day approaches, you will hear the telltale flappings as each exercises its wings in the nest box in preparation for that first clumsy plunge into the outside world. Each chick has gone through the necessary slimming phase, which you will have noted as the parents' demand for food decreases about a week before fledging. The

Above: Pearl chicks ranging in age from 14 to 18 days. **Below:** A good comparison of youngsters: a Cinnamon Pearl and a Pearl. **Facing page:** Pied Cockatiel. Photos by Horst Bielfeld.

chick would be unable to fly if it kept that pendulous crop and otherwise unstreamlined proportions of infancy. Each chick will spend time peeking out of the nest-box hole, inspecting the big world beyond. One can imagine the finality of fledging in the wild: should the chick fly too far and become separated, or not learn quickly enough to attain perching height, or be unable to follow the parents, its weeks of growth would all be in vain. Fortunately, in captivity the chances of its demise at this point are slimmer, the weak ones having probably succumbed earlier. Also it is unlikely that it can, in a cage or flight, be far from its parents' attentions. It's a sign of weakness or immaturity if a chick does not learn to climb or fly to a perch within 24 hours—for instance, the youngest of a large clutch leaving the nest at the same time as its older siblings. It has probably been underfed or has not sufficiently developed, and so cannot summon the strength to achieve this instinctive goal. Chances are, the parents will attend to its feeding, even at floor level, and the chick will eventually escape its plight. In the wild, the chick would surely have died. You might return it to the nest box.

Despite handling in the nest box, the young, when they first leave the nest, are extremely nervous. They are not only unfamiliar with their suddenly vast and strange surroundings, but they lack the dexterity in flying and most especially in landing properly. For a few days, any sudden movement by you, while carrying out your chores, may result in sudden and complete panic on their part. This too will pass, probably without injury. A steady pair of parents will help through example to allay their fears.

Chances are, the hen is already beginning to lay a new clutch while all, or the youngest, of the chicks are still in the nest box. This is what makes it so difficult to split up a pair at your discretion after two good nests. The hen must be allowed to complete her egg laying, and you must either foster the eggs out to another hen or just throw the eggs out. Do not overwork your breeding pair.

Amazingly enough, the eggs are usually not broken, despite the numerous boarders in the nest box. The biggest danger is that the eggs may become encrusted with droppings, diminishing the air exchange through the shell. Occasionally, you might have to very gently clean the eggs with warm water, softening the feces enough to be wiped off or delicately picked off. The egg does not have to be spotless.

WEANING. Meanwhile, as the hen resumes incubation, the male will be feeding the fledged chicks, gradually teaching them by example to find food themselves. At this point it is most important to keep the cage or flight floor as clean as possible, as the chicks will begin to peck at anything in sight, including droppings if these are more prevalent than food.

Seed should be scattered loose on the floor, and extra seed dishes placed so they won't be soiled from perches overhead. The chicks eventually will become accustomed to your one regular feeding station, so this is only a temporary measure. All kinds of food (not just seed) should be offered, as well as a surplus of those seeds which are easiest to husk: canary, spray millet, oats, and soaked or sprouted seed mixes. With experience, the young will graduate to the more difficult seeds like sunflower and hemp. Now is the time, while they are in the experimenting phase, to encourage and cultivate a wide range of tastes. Finicky birds, no matter their pedigree, seldom develop to their full potential and, if eventually bred, will not in turn feed a variety of foods to their own young.

About a week after leaving the nest box, you will begin to see the fledglings, now more adept at flying, following the parent, begging to be fed and, most importantly, starting to peck at the food alongside the adult. The male will continue to feed the chicks while the hen incubates the next clutch, but gradually he turns a deaf ear to their entreaties as they learn to consume enough to finally become independent. Allow at least two weeks for weaning from the time the young leave the nest box (the chicks will by no be approximately seven to eight weeks old). Hopefully, the adult male can have

Above: Two hen Cockatiels: the lighter one is a Cinnamon Pearl, the other a Pearl. Photo by Dale R. Thompson and George D. Dodge. **Facing page:** A Cinnamon bird in company with what has been referred to as "Lavenderwing," a variant of the Lutino mutation. Photo by Michael ·Gilroy.

a few days' rest from feeding young before the second clutch begins to hatch. Observe the weanlings as they feed: are they merely mouthing the seed or actually husking it? They will not be adept yet at the art of hulling each seed with split-second timing, but as long as they have learned how, their skill will increase with experience.

Catch up the weaned babies (possibly leaving the younger one of a large clutch for a few more days) and place them in a separate cage or flight; still watch carefully for the next day or two to be sure that each chick is sustaining itself. Provide both water bottles and dishes of water. Any baby that is puffed up on the floor must be immediately returned to the parents, as it is not completely weaned. Do not necessarily take sleeping on a perch to mean insufficient feeding. Young Cockatiels, like all babies, sleep more than adults. If available, a pet or steady adult bird should be placed with the recently separated young to further encourage the chicks to eat. Occasionally you may find an adult that will actually feed the unrelated weanlings. Such an adult is worth its weight in gold, as you can separate the young earlier and use him or her to teach the chicks, thus saving the breeding male's energies for the next nest. Using a pet, or otherwise steady bird, will also help to calm the newly independent chicks. A new cage or flight will probably set them in a dither all over again for a few days, until they become familiar with the surroundings.

Once young birds are fully self-sufficient and able to be sexed accurately, they can be placed in the adult male or female flights. Watch that each is not unduly picked on, especially in the male pen where there may be aggressive adults in breeding condition. It is ideal to have separate flights for young males and females. The sexually undetermined young must continue to be kept separate until the young males become obvious at about three to four months of age by their whistlings, or the hens by their lack of vocal performance.

HOW-TO'S

Banding

Banding a bird is the best method for identifying each individual bird. This can be achieved by either of two types of bands: closed or open. Closed bands must be placed on the leg of the hatchling, so that as the baby grows, the band becomes permanent identification. His joints will quickly develop to a point that the band cannot be removed short of actual cutting off the metal ring, or the leg itself. Open bands can be placed on birds at any age and can also be removed by easier means; thus they are not considered to be positive proof of age or breeder identification. However, should you purchase a bird that bears no band, applying an open band is a way for you to identify it in your records, along with your "home raised" close-banded birds.

A further aid in identification is using a different colored band for each year. Then you can at a glance identify birds of a certain age (green was '86, orange '87, etc.) without having to catch them. (The American Cockatiel Society offers registered, color-coded bands to club members.) Another trick is to band your birds on the right leg one year, then on the left the next year (don't ask me what happens the third year, as I haven't used this method).

For a singly kept pet a band is not important, nor with a single pair of breeders, as long as the babies are separated before they become indistinguishable from the parents (the two long central tail flights, before they are fully grown, being the best way to distinguish the young from the adult hen). Yet, even with a single pair of breeders, banding may be use-

Above: Two Lutino Pearl nestlings. The degree of pearling will vary. I would suspect the chick facing is a male; the other, more heavily pearled, is probably a hen. Photo by Nancy A. Reed.

Facing page: Two Lutino Pearls. This is a beautiful cross-mutation, showing more yellow coloration than a Lutino. However, as in any variety involving the Pearl factor, adult males will eventually lose their "lacings." With this cross-mutation, they will look like plain Lutinos; but they are still valuable for breeding because they can always pass on the Pearl gene. Photo by Horst Bielfeld.

ful to establish the precise age of the young or to distinguish the first clutch from the second, etc. However, as bands are usually purchased in minimum lots of 25, you might prefer to use open bands for this purpose or to mark the birds with mercurochrome or lipstick, or to house each clutch separately in different cages or flights.

There are two bad aspects of banding: (1) the possibility that the band might become caught on an exposed wire-end in the flight or even a twig stump (be constantly aware of such potential hazards when constructing your flights or replacing branches); (2) if the banded leg is somehow injured, it may become swollen to the point that the band hampers circulation to the foot. Such accidents are infrequent, but when they do happen, you curse the necessity of using bands simply for your ease in keeping records. There are band-cutting scissors; but if a bird's leg has become swollen to the point that the band should be removed, one can sometimes have a hair-raising time trying to cut the band. (Fortunately, in the cases I've had, the swelling was reduced before the band became a tourniquet.)

However, in the long run, banding is a must, not only to record age, but most especially to keep track of the pedigrees for future breeding pairings (and for adult Pearl males that revert to normal coloration and then can no longer be identified visually). Once the sex of a bird becomes apparent and so noted in your records, his or her individual number will be all that is needed for assurance when catching up that particular bird. If a bird should be lost or stolen, positive identification and proof of ownership can be established.

CLOSED BANDS. These are "identification bracelets," with an inside diameter of approximately one-quarter inch, have one digit and one initial to designate the breeder and another number to specify the bird (04, 39, 540, etc.), followed by two digits representing the year of hatching ('86, '87, etc.) The American Cockatiel Society issues bands that include your registered personal identification code (4R, 2S, 7D, etc.) along with numbers for the bird and the year; each band is also stamped with "A.C.S.". Therefore any bird bearing an A.C.S. band can be easily traced and identified through the Society's records.

Aside from the purposes stated above, banding is also necessary for shows that offer unflighted (young) classes. Eligible for this class are *closed* banded birds bearing the number and color of the present year; in other words, birds under one year of age.

A closed band must be put on the chick's leg while the ankle joint is still small enough for the ring to pass over it— usually between eight and fourteen days of age. One can judge the timing at a glance: the crest feathers will be starting to erupt on the bird's forehead. Should the bird be small, the band may slide with no resistance forward over the ankle joint, and it may subsequently be lost in the nest box. Always check such birds for a few days after banding to be sure the band is in place. On the other hand, if the bird is large for its age, petroleum jelly or soap may be needed for lubrication in easing the band over an ankle that is almost too large. There is about three to four days leeway for banding. Sometimes two or maybe three chicks from the same clutch may be banded at the same time, but one must be careful that banding does not become impossible through your tardiness and the chick's fast growth.

Before describing the actual physical maneuvers of banding, let me state Rule No. 1: hold the bird over a counter, table, etc. Many babies have been injured or killed when, with a sudden squirm, they have accidentally fallen to the floor. Another precaution is to hold the bird in such a manner so as not to put pressure on the probably bulging crop. Avoid the possibility of the food being squeezed back up into the throat and choking the bird. Also do not hold the bird's body in such a viselike grip that it cannot breathe; the chick is delicate and does not need any great force to be restrained.

One can hold the chick with bare hands, as it will not bite. Have your band ready (right side up), along with a toothpick

Lutino Pearl Cockatiel. Photo by Horst Bielfeld.

and lubricant, should the latter be needed. The bird will be small enough to cradle in one hand while the fingers of the same hand hold the foot in position. Move the longer back toe forward to meet the two front toes, the shorter back toe remaining behind. With your free hand, place the band over these three forward toes, sliding the band the length of the toes and finally over the ankle joint. The short back toe will probably have to be pried out from under the band with a toothpick or some other slender implement. The band will now be in proper place on the leg between the ankle and knee joints. Give a slight tug forward to see if the ankle and toes provide enough resistance to keep the band in place. If it is obvious that the band will slip off too easily, it is better to remove it and wait another day or two before trying again. Otherwise, the band may be lost in the litter of the nest box, and you may not notice in time. This will automatically cause the bird to become the best creature you ever raised, but without a band ineligible for exhibition.

Promptly make notes in your records of each bird's band number. Each bird is now permanently identifiable, an individual that can be sought out with certainty in the future.

While in the nest, the bands on the chicks' feet will become encrusted with droppings, but by the time you will be checking the bands for identification (i.e., after the bird has fledged and is weaned), the band will again be clean.

OPEN BANDS. Open bands are used as an alternate means to identify birds that have not been closed banded. They cannot be used as proof of age, as they may be affixed to any bird, be he two weeks, two years, or twenty years of age. Thus the year number is usually omitted when ordering, and the band will include only the breeder's initials and and a number for the bird. A minimum order of 25 bands can therefore be useful for a number of years to identify either new stock that has been purchased and has not been closed banded, or for youngsters that have somehow been skipped over and are too old for closed banding. These birds will not be eligible for

BANDING A CHICK is generally done at 7–14 days of age, depending on the size of the chick.

Move the longer back toe forward.

Hold the three longest toes together.

Slip the closed band over the three toes.

Push the band up over the joint. If the fit is tight, using petroleum jelly or soap for lubrication will help.

The smaller back toe must be flipped out of the band. A toothpick or any small pointed implement can be placed between the toe and the leg to pull the toe gently out from under the band.

The band should remain on the leg between the foot and the hock joint. Test by pulling the band over the foot. If it slips off easily, wait a day or two until the chick has grown more.

unflighted classes at shows despite the fact that you know they are birds of the year. Open bands are useful solely as a means of identification for *your* records.

Open banding an adult bird can occasionally cause minor problems, as an older bird is bothered far more than a chick by the new bracelet, and may chew and fiddle with the band to the extent that the leg becomes irritated or actually bloody. This is not common, but should such a situation arise, the band may have to be removed by immobilizing the bird in a towel or with a glove, and carefully prying the band far enough open to be removed. It is because of this ability to remove or replace open bands that they cannot be considered as proof positive of a bird's age or origin.

Open bands are identical in size to closed bands, but are cut at one point and therefore can be spread wide in order to be placed over the leg immediately above the ankle joint. A special banding tool (or even pliers) can then be used to squeeze the band closed again so that it will not fall off, so it can be considered semi-permanent. When reclosing the band, be sure that the opening's edges are aligned, i.e., a sharp corner is not sticking out, above, or below the smooth ring that the band should form. Any such points could be irritating and cause an unnecessary wound.

This banding process sounds much more complicated in words than it is in action. I am merely pointing out all precautions against possible problems.

Watch the newly banded bird for a few days to be sure that it adjusts to its new anklet without irritating its leg with too much attention. It will spend a bit of time being annoyed, but will usually adapt to the encumbrance shortly and with no further problems.

Hand-Feeding

Before delving into the subject of hand-feeding, it must be emphasized that the most important qualification you need for the job is dedication. Depending on the age at which you start hand-feeding the chicks, plan ahead, for you will be tied down for several weeks.

When one decides to tackle the chore (and hand-feeding *is* a chore), you must also be the patient sort, taking the time every few hours to play "parent bird." If you want to go to Uncle Harry's house for the weekend, guess who goes with you? Have no fears—the little ones are excellent travelers, whether by land or air.

Also realize that you may not be successful on your first try. It is heartbreaking and frustrating to lose a little fellow you have nurtured so carefully. For some reason, hand-fed Cockatiels seem to be more prone to digestive upsets than other psittacines. When the condition cannot be remedied, you watch, defeated, as the chick gets worse and finally dies. When this happens you vow, "Never again!"—but you will.

Why Choose Hand-Feeding? First, let's discuss when it is necessary to hand-feed.

When the parents fail to carry out their rearing duties, it may be necessary to hand-feed for one of the following reasons: (1) If the parent birds are too young, they may not be reliable enough to finish what they started. (2) The parents start another clutch when the youngest being reared is under two weeks of age. (3) Something has caused the parent birds to become unsettled: they were not conditioned to your looking in the nest box; strangers; unusual noises; changes in their location or environment. If the parents are extremely disturbed, they may abandon or kill the chicks. (4) One of the parents dies. Remember, Cockatiels share in the rearing of young, and one bird alone cannot be expected to finish rearing a large clutch. (5) For some reason the parents reject a chick. (It may be a weakling, and may not respond to hand-feeding either.)

If you cannot transfer the chicks to another nest box with young because of one of the above reasons, and you want to save the chicks, hand-feeding becomes a necessity. When you do transfer chicks to another box, put them in with young of similar size and color. You may encounter problems putting Normals under Lutinos, etc., or vice versa. Birds can't count, but sometimes they will not accept color changes.

Alternatively, you may hand-feed by choice. A hand-fed Cockatiel makes an "instant" pet, and this is ideal for someone who lacks the patience or skill to tame a "wild" bird for a pet. Many a would-be pet becomes a forlorn ornament because it did not hop right on the new owner's hand when first introduced.

Having a super pet to give as a gift or to sell is reward enough for all the work, when the recipient repeatedly tells you how happy he or she is with your hand-fed baby.

You may want to keep the best of a hand-fed brood as a potential show bird or future breeder. Even if allowed to "go wild" after weaning, the bird will, when caught up, be easier to train for showing and will not be a nervous, flighty parent during nesting.

WHEN TO FEED. The ideal age to take young from the nest to be fed is around 16 to 19 days old. The pin feathers will cover the body, and some flight feathers will start to break open at the tips. At this age they are not too delicate or overly frightened.

An older, fully feathered chick can prove somewhat difficult to convert to hand-feeding. For a day or two he must be force-fed until he finally recognizes that you truly have his best interest in mind and in hand.

The best time of day to take the young from the nest box is just before the birds settle down for the night and the babies' crops are bulging. By morning, your new charges' crops will be empty, and the birds will be more receptive to your style of breakfast.

HOW MANY CHICKS TO FEED. It is not advisable to hand-feed just one chick. Not only does it need the warmth and support of its siblings, but if you are going to all the trouble of heating up the formula, it takes only a moment to feed a few more mouths.

It is best to take two from the nest initially and then another one each day. This is less upsetting to the parents, and, if you should run into problems in learning the knack of hand-feeding, the babies can be returned to the nest and the parents will still be disposed to continue. Also, each new addition to your group will hear the eager squeaks of its already "trained" siblings and therefore be more willing to try this new-fangled arrangement. If problems arise, don't wait until the chicks are dying before returning them to their parents. They must still be strong enough to beg. If they don't beg to be fed, the parents won't feed them.

Let the parents raise at least half, if not all of the first clutch each year. This keeps them in practice, so they don't get the notion that they will not have to feed chicks the full term. Otherwise, if you have a problem, you won't be able to return the chicks to the parents.

WHERE TO HOUSE HAND-FED CHICKS. If the birds are under five weeks of age, place them in either an extra nest box or a carton of similar size. If they are not sufficiently feathered to maintain body heat, you must supply additional warmth by placing a heating pad under the box, use a hospital cage, or place a low-wattage light bulb in a second box of the same size beneath the box containing the chicks. Do not allow the temperature to exceed 80° F. Don't guess! Place a thermometer in the bedding material or on the surface. This is a most critical factor for success. If you are hand-feeding three or more babies, older than 14 or 16 days, you shouldn't have to add any heat. If the room is cool, place a light-weight towel over the box (if it has no top) to help hold the heat in. Too much heat is one of four factors causing sour crop, the other three factors being overfeeding, sour food, or too rich a diet.

How Much to Feed. The frequency and amount you feed is also very important, and should be adjusted to the bird's age. In chicks under a week of age, the crop is tiny and cannot hold much food. Therefore, it is necessary to feed a little, but often, every two to four hours. Chicks younger than two weeks may require having a 2 A.M. feeding for safety's sake. It is truly a Herculean feat to raise such a tiny, delicate hatchling. After two weeks of age, it may take from four to six hours before the crop is empty. At this stage you can feed just before your bedtime (10 or 11 P.M.), and the chicks should be just fine until breakfast (6 or 7 A.M.). After three or four weeks of age, a feeding every eight hours should be sufficient.

It is best to let the crop empty before filling it again. Keeping a baby constantly full will contribute to sour crop. If the room is cool, a chick will use more food to keep warm; during warm weather, less food is needed. So fill the babies only ⅔ to ¾ full, and allow the crop to empty before feeding again.

One frequent rejoinder is "But this isn't the way the parents feed." True, but every time they feed, they are giving extra digestive juices to the babies to help the food go through. You don't.

Under normal conditions, you shouldn't ever force them to eat more than they want. If they start playing or don't want any more food, *quit*—they will be that much hungrier next time. Most Cockatiels are aggressive eaters and have to be cut off once in awhile.

About the fifth week, you will notice a lot of wing exercise. The chicks are preparing to leave the nest box. This is one period when you will have trouble feeding, and it is important not to force the food. The chicks become more interested in what's going on around the room and often play with the food. There is an explanation for this behavior. Nature has provided them with the instinct not only to exercise for flight, but also to trim down in weight for their first flying lesson.

WHAT TO FEED. This is indeed a difficult subject to write on. If you ask 42 experienced and successful "hand-feeders" what each one's proven procedure and formula is, you will get 42 different routines and recipes. Different people will advise different temperatures for an artificial brooder. How often to feed seems to be a point of contention too, but I tend to go along with the idea of checking every few hours and feeding as needed (when crop is empty). Everyone agrees that overfeeding may be harmful.

A newly hatched chick must have a simple food. Mix oatmeal or high-protein baby cereal with warm water to the consistency of gravy, perhaps adding one drop of milk per teaspoon of formula for a chick under five days of age.

Before we go further, Rule No. 1 states is that the food must always be warm! Remember that the mixture will cool quickly unless you keep the food container in a pan of very warm water. After the chick is four to five days old, you can add to the mixture to make it more nutritious. Good additions are sunflower meal and millet meal, which can be purchased at health food stores. Marie Olssen used 1 tbs. sunflower meal, 3 tbs. millet meal, 4 tbs. high-protein baby cereal, and enough water to make it thin enough to feed. At about one week of age, add a drop or two of vitamins. Also at about one week, a teaspoon of garden- or mixed-vegetable strained baby food may be added.

The late Mrs. Moon, the "Mother" of Cockatiels here in the U.S., was truly a good hen. She went as far as to chew up nestling food, or oatmeal and hulled sunflower seeds, herself. When all was moist and warm, she would feed mouth to mouth, or with her finger. This was fine for a quick feed to a nestling that needed a little pick-me-up. However, for a whole brood of hungry chicks, it seems a bit impractical. She then used quick-cook rolled oats, a little powdered or canned milk, and added dry nestling food for proper consistency. Or if she was in a hurry and had no time to cook the oats, she used Pabulum or flaky baby cereals from the box.

Dee Dee Squyres in Texas has hand-fed everything from Budgies to macaws, and with good results. She has kindly contributed the following formula. This recipe obviously makes a large amount. It is suggested that it be stored in several small containers and frozen. When kept in the refrigerator, servings will last three days.

Squyres's Formula
⅔ cup Hi-Protein baby cereal (dry flakes)
⅓ cup Purina Monkey Chow (ground in blender)
½ cup Wheathearts
1 cup sunflower meal
½ cup hulled or ground millet
¼ cup ground raw peanuts
1 jar (7¾ oz.) oatmeal, applesauce, and banana baby food
1 jar (4½ oz.) strained corn baby food
1 jar (3⅓ oz.) egg yolk baby food

Put all ingredients together in a large bowl. Add water for mixing. Then take two cupfuls at a time and run through a blender at high speed. Add water as necessary to make a very liquid mixture. As the formula sets it will thicken. For feeding, combine this mixture with an equal amount of high-protein baby cereal and blend, adding enough water to produce a soupy consistency. Finally, add 1 tsp. of milk per 5 oz. of formula.

At feeding time, remember again Rule No. 1: *Food must be warm* (a birds' temperature is 104° F.). Put a couple of spoonfuls (depending how much is needed for one feeding) of formula in a small container and heat. If the mixture is too hot, the bird will shake its head. If it is too cold and the bird, especially a very young chick, is forced to eat it, it can upset digestion.

Dry mixes which have been especially formulated for hand-rearing are now commercially available.

WITH WHAT TO FEED. Use either a tiny baby spoon (long handled and approximately ½ tsp. in size) or a regular spoon with sides bent to form a scoop. However, I personally prefer an eyedropper. Sometimes the outlet must be enlarged to allow the formula through easily. I prefer it to a spoon because I can squirt the food directly into the crop. This helps to convince a chick that the whole strange process does actually work. Many people use the commercially available Handi-feeder, a syringe-type implement designed for hand-feeding. My only complaint is that it takes two hands to refill it, so one must put the chick down. Fine for one baby, but with a whole squawking bunch, it's a bit tedious for all concerned. And what a raspy chorus follows as they beg, "Me first, me first!"

HOW TO FEED. Now for the messy part: trying to get more food into the chick than on, under, or around it. In the nest the parent birds lock their beaks with the babies', and all shake vigorously as the food is regurgitated from the adults' crops into the babies' throats. This instinctive jerking of your little charge can prove most frustrating and messy! Sometimes it is necessary to hold the chick's head between your thumb and forefinger in order to get the eyedropper into the mouth and squirt the food on target. Marie Olssen showed me a little trick of wrapping a cloth around the chick's neck, like a bib, so that the food does not end up all over the feathers. However, my hand-fed babies always end up looking like a floor mop used in a glue factory, no matter how hard I try.

Assuming your formula has been made in advance, spoon out enough for one feeding. If the babies are very small, or you only have one bird to feed, place the food in a small dish (such as an egg-poacher cup) and sit it on a coffee mug that has been filled with scalding hot water from the faucet. When feeding a large clutch (three weeks old or more), you can put the food in a 4 oz. baby-food jar, place it in a pan of water, and heat the formula on the stove. (Microwave ovens are super time savers.) While the food is warming, set up a

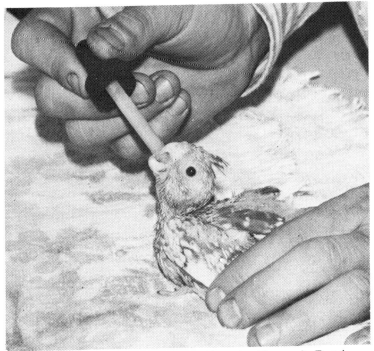

Handfeeding a Cockatiel nestling. Photo by Nancy A. Reed.

bowl of warm water in the sink, with a rag or washcloth close by for cleaning up the chick after feeding. Also put a paper towel or tissue down for the chick to stand on while being fed. Have a box of tissues handy for drying off the chick after washing. The formula is probably ready now. Stir well and test the temperature on the tip of your tongue. Keep the pan of hot water close by in case the food cools down before all are fed.

Now place the chick on the towel, holding the bird gently around its shoulders to restrain and control the eager eater's wiggling (or when the chick is tiny, hold it in your hand). If this is the chick's first experience, you may have to coax it a bit by allowing some warm food to seep into the side of the mouth. This is often enough for a young chick to catch on and open wide. An older baby can be more stubborn. Fortunately, the good Lord must have foreseen such a situation, as the sides of the lower mandible are designed to extend out slightly from the upper. This makes a perfect little ledge to place the end of an eyedropper or spoon on and then force down upon, so that the mouth will open and you can quickly scoot some goodies in. Usually after a few such urgings the chick will get the idea and open wide.

With an older baby that is fully feathered, you can have quite a time. Then it is sometimes necessary to force the beak open with thumb and finger in each side, holding it open so that the dropper can be forced in and food deposited. Care should be taken so that in the course of the struggle, no food is ejected into the windpipe instead of the crop. This could result in pneumonia and probably the demise of the bird. Quick squirts of food with dropper *deep* into the throat is the best precaution against this. Force-feeding may be necessary for several meals, until the chick gives in and cooperates. This is not a pleasant experience for either you or the bird; but fight, force, and convince you must, or the bird starves.

Except for these initial feedings, your little charges should soon become more than eager to be fed. After the chick's crop is about full, wash its face and breast (this is easy until feathers grow), dry it well with a tissue, and pop the contented bird back into its box or cage. Stir the food again, check its temperature, then proceed with the next baby. When all are fed, clean all utensils, with special attention to rinsing out the eyedropper thoroughly.

GOOD HOUSEKEEPING. Cleanliness in the nest box and cage is important. With all the soft food going in one end, the results from the other are copious and very messy. Such droppings from an adult bird might be a sign of illness and cause for alarm. In hand-fed babies, this "diarrhea" is normal. Bedding must be changed often. You can use Litter Green, wood shavings, tissues etc., in the nest box when birds are under five weeks of age. I use several layers of paper toweling for older birds in a cage. (One should have stock in a paper company for all the rolls of towels and boxes of tissues one uses when hand-feeding.) Babies will start picking at bedding even when still in the nest box, so cleanliness is an obvious necessity.

CROP PROBLEMS. Hopefully, you will raise the brood to independence with no problems. However, always be on the alert for signs of sour or compacted crop. These are the most common problems and are usually the result of overfeeding (assuming your food is not spoiled, your chicks and formula are warm enough, and the mix is not too rich). The chicks, in their eagerness, don't seem to know when to stop eating. Their crops are bulging, but they keep begging, and the urge to give more food is tempting. Don't! Often an eyedropperful or spoonful of warm water is enough to satisfy them. The best policy is always to feed a little, but often.

The warning symptom for sour crop is a pumping action of the head and neck from side to side in an effort to regurgitate. Or the baby will constantly hold his head high and, if not feathered out, food can be seen going up and down in the esophagus from the crop. The crop will also still be full at the next feeding.

With a compacted crop, the food has become hard and won't move. (Perhaps the formula may have been too dry.) The bird's crop remains full between feedings, and although he acts hungry, he will only take a small amount.

I have had partial success (you win some, you lose some) in treating both maladies. Immediately put distressed birds on heat (or more heat). There are two courses to try, or a combination of the two. If the crop remains full, it is best to empty it manually. This is more easily done with sour crop. Hold the bird upside down and *gently* squeeze the crop from the bottom, working towards the mouth (like squeezing a tube of toothpaste). Remember that the bird must breathe, so do this quickly and repeatedly, but with pauses in between. If the bird will take some warm water after the initial emptying, you can effectively wash the crop out.

With a compacted crop (depending how hard the lump is), the same sort of manipulation sometimes alleviates the problem. If possible, give the bird some warm water, then massage the crop, trying to work the water into the mass to soften it. Then try emptying the crop manually. If too compacted, a tiny bit of mineral oil will sometimes lubricate the contents and allow it to pass on to the stomach.

The second course entails the use of Sal Hepatica, a mild laxative to wash "the pipes" out. This comes in powder form and can be purchased at a drugstore. Buy some Pepto Bismol (a liquid) also, as we follow up with this to coat and soothe the crop. These medicines may be used following manual emptying or, if the crop is almost empty, as the sole remedy.

Mix ½ tsp. Sal Hepatica to a pint of warm water, or a tiny pinch to ¼ cup of warm water and feed some to the baby. Wait three hours and use the same proportions with Pepto Bismol. Then wait three hours and try your regular hand-feeding formula. Feed a little, often, until bird is back to normal and the crop empties between meals.

LEAVING THE NEST. Around four to five weeks of age your babies will become seemingly unappreciative of your labors. They will eat a bit and then become more interested in their surroundings than in their heretofore "beloved" eyedropper or spoon. This is a natural development. They must start to slim down if they are to fly. Under the feathers, the crop is no longer the ponderous pouch it was. You will also hear them exercising their wings in the nest box, preparing for their maiden flights. At this point you will graduate them to a cage (simulating their leaving the nest in nature).

Also, after about four weeks of age, you will notice the chicks' appetites in the morning are lagging. Late-afternoon or evening meals, or both, are their favorites. I have also observed this in the parent birds' feeding practices, as babies may still be without breakfast by 9:00 in the morning.

Weaning

Once out of the nest box, we reach the final stage: weaning. I shouldn't even be writing this part as I am the world's worst weaner. One can have a hard time turning a deaf ear to a begging baby, and I have ended up hand-feeding as long as four months—ridiculous, but true! Chicks can wrap me around their little toes. Well, perhaps I can tell you what you are *supposed* to do.

The cage floor should have seed, Petamine, and gravel (optional) spread around liberally. Containers (except for water) are not desirable at this point, as the birds' natural instincts are to pick at the ground like chickens. (While hand-feeding you can help to promote this inclination by lowering the eyedropper or spoon so they are eating at ground level.) Sunflower seed is too difficult for them to husk at first, so I either crack a handful with a rolling pin or use leftovers from my parrots' or adult Cockatiels' food dishes. The older birds leave many bits of the sunflower seed.

Considerable seed will be wasted because the floor of the cage must be cleaned so often, but don't skimp on food. Also, variety is good. Besides the parakeet mix, millet sprays are easy for babies to husk, as is canary seed (add some extra to the regular mix). Whole-wheat bread softened with water or milk, greens, uncooked corn cut off the cob (or canned or frozen), fruit, and soaked seed are all easy for the chicks to eat. One can even put some hand-feeding formula in a jar lid (and hope they don't just walk in it or play with the lid itself). But remember to replace within a few hours anything that will spoil or wilt.

A tame or steady adult Cockatiel, placed in with the babies, can be a big help. The young will learn by noticing the older bird's interest in foods and how he husks seeds.

At this stage, you cannot abruptly cease hand-feeding. The birds gradually learn the art of hulling their own seed. At first, they are able only to feed themselves enough for you to

cut out the noontime feeding. Gradually you can omit breakfast, but the late afternoon or evening meal remains the most
important. Don't send a bird to bed on an empty stomach.

Eventually, the birds will only accept a few swallows of
formula when it is offered, and you will know they are eating
enough on their own. But remember, if you are feeding a
large brood, that the youngest can be as much as two weeks
behind the oldest. Some will be weaned but others will still
need a bit of help.

If birds have been promised to new homes, wait a week to
make sure they are doing fine on their own. If they will be
shipped, you should wait longer. But keep handling the
birds. Otherwise, once they are weaned, they will quite
quickly forget what a great guy you were when they needed
you most. Those you reserve as breeders or show birds may
not forever jump on your finger, but they will usually remain
"steady" birds. I have caught up adults that had been hand-
fed and have been loose in flights for several years, and although they are unhappy at being handled, they will not bite
the hand that once fed them—so very conscientiously.

(My sincere thanks to Vern Bright, who has had far more
experience and success than I have in this area. Besides his
suggestions, much of the writing of the foregoing part of this
chapter must be credited to him. My appreciation also ex-
tends to those people who are mentioned by name, for their
contributions.)

Sexing
Being able to determine the sex of a Cockatiel is not only obviously important in pairing birds for breeding but for select-
ing pets for those who desire specifically a male or a female
bird. Unfortunately, sexing young birds is not always an easy
feat, nor can one be expected to be correct a hundred percent
of the time, especially with those mutations which are difficult to sex. However, there are signs that, if not completely
reliable on young birds, are good indicators in adults.

THE PELVIC TEST. Pelvic testing is considered the most universal test for all species of birds—the hen having a wider space between the pelvic bones to accommodate the passage of eggs, while (in Cockatiels) the male's pelvic points are just short of touching. Personally, I do not rely principally on this feature, especially in young birds, as the bones are then so pliable and therefore variable that a chick can be thought to be a male one day and decidedly a female the next. Even in older birds it can be deceptive. On a breeding pair it becomes quite accurate, but who needs to test then? However, pelvic testing should not be completely discounted, as some females will always have widely set bones, and some males' pelvic points will remain very close. But again, there are always those other males or females that do not display the obvious extremes.

Holding the bird in a natural, horizontal position, the points of the pelvic bones are located approximately ½ inch forward of the bird's vent, toward the breast. They are the only bones in that area below the rib cage (which is located about 1½ inches from the vent) and feel quite obvious as "points" when touched. The pelvic bones of a female would be far enough apart that the thickness of a pencil could fit between them. A male's pelvic bones, on the other hand, would almost touch or have a separation of only ⅛ inch.

Even though the pelvic-bone method might be fairly accurate, it is best to use this test only in conjunction with other signs before making a final judgment.

CHICKS AND YOUNG BIRDS. The only time that chicks can be positively sexed while still in the nest is when they are the progeny of a few specific crosses, e.g., a Lutino, Pearl, or Cinnamon male mated to a Normal hen. All young showing the coloration (mutation) of the father are hens; all Normal (gray) babies are males and split for the father's mutation.

However, with most crosses, one must wait until well after weaning, at about three months of age, when the male youngsters will begin their trial whistlings and warblings. By *warblings* I mean a bird that sounds like a first-year music student just starting to learn the flute. An adult male Cockie will often have his own personal "song," but a young male will experiment: no set pattern and thus much variation until he perfects what he will call his song. A flight of these young males sounds much like the local symphony orchestra warming up. This is hard to explain, but once you hear it, you will recognize what I am trying to describe. Do not decide that a bird is a male simply on the basis of an initial performance, as there is always that singular female that will perform in such a fashion. But try to remember the bird by noting some special physical characteristic or the band number on the leg as it perches. Usually, when I separate the brood from their parents, I will mark an under-tail flight feather on each bird with mercurochrome or a felt-tip marker (one dot, two dots, one dash, two dashes, etc.), so that I can identify each chick by sight more easily. Then continue to observe them. If the bird persists in chortling often and over a period of several weeks, it is a 90% bet that it's a male. The pelvic test can now be used to further confirm your hunch. A small mirror, placed at the end of a perch, will sometimes encourage the males to initiate their "singing" earlier or more noticeably.

The next sign will become evident in Normal, Pearl, Cinnamon, Fallow, and White-Face males at four to six months of age: the characteristic yellow feathers around the face begin to appear.

In summary (excepting the auto-sexing young from some crosses), to sex young one must rely on male mannerisms (and the lack of such vocalization in hens), the pelvic test, and the onset of the male coloration of some varieties.

ADOLESCENT AND ADULT BIRDS. On the Normal, Cinnamon, Fallow, and Whiteface, the adolescent males become obvious (as they mature) by the ever-increasing yellow "mask," and the eventual loss of the yellow-barred-with-gray undertail characteristic of females and immatures. The differences between the sexes in these two Cockatiel varieties are certainly clear by breeding age.

Pearls take a bit longer to become evident. Every male Pearl as he begins to mature will start to lose his spots, and by breeding age will look like a Normal adult male, retaining perhaps a few telltale markings or "tickings." Often the bird will end up a deeper gray-to-black than the usual Normal male.

The Lutino mutation is the next most difficult to sex, but this is possible visually, especially when the bird is more than a year old. Do not rely on cheek-patch brightness for males! (This is true for other varieties as well.) The best indication is the lack of barring on wing and tail flights in adult male Lutinos, but remember that a year-old bird will not necessarily have molted all of these flight feathers. Note the triangular patch of feathers radiating from the vent, terminating at a point and covering the base of the tail flights (the under tail coverts). In a female, these will all be barred yellow-and-white; a male will be colored solid, or "flat," here (white or yellow). A young male, after the six-months' molt, will display at least a few of these solid-colored feathers.

On Lutinos, it is best to catch the bird and check it at close range under good lighting, as the yellow barring or spotting is usually very subtle on the white background of the feather.

I have also found that male Lutinos are more prone to baldness and usually carry a lesser amount of yellow suffusion on the breast and back feathers. In other words, they appear whiter, although the adult male's head may end up a deeper yellow.

Pieds are the most difficult to sex. There are no regular plumage differences between the sexes. Here one must rely mainly on the characteristic male mannerisms: whistlings and strutting.

As I have never worked with Pieds, I assumed that any flight feathers would show the characteristic yellow spots on hens, or the lack thereof on males. This I have been advised is not necessarily totally accurate, but it might be used with an adult bird as an *indication* of sex when considered along with mannerisms and the pelvic test.

Finally, may I say once more that the male's display is probably one's best criterion for sexing, especially in a young bird that is not fully colored.

Patience on the part of both the breeder and the buyer offers the best guarantee of accurate sexing. This will minimize any slighting of the breeder's reputation and eventual disappointment to the buyer. Any purchaser demanding a very young bird (usually for a pet), must be made fully aware that the breeder's "educated guess" is no more than that. If sex is not vitally important, fine. But remember that Cockatiels are noted for their tractability, and even a three to six-month-old, sexable bird should not be beyond the average person's taming ability.

Shipping

Transporting birds can become an important consideration to the breeder who produces many birds. In fact, shipping is often a necessity; unless you live in a well-populated and bird-loving area, your aviaries will before long reach the saturation point. When I first started breeding the Cinnamons and Pearls, I was worried that local clientele were basically interested only in Normal and Lutino Cockatiels. They were not familiar or interested in the newer and more expensive mutations. If I wanted to continue and improve these rarer varieties, I would have to expand my marketing in order to make room. A breeder will usually sell 90% of each year's young, keeping only the "pick of the litters" for furthering his own goals.

Many people frown on shipping birds. Yes, there is a risk involved, and I know the birds themselves are not enthralled with the whole process. I did have a very rare experience: a pair of Cockatiels were stolen out of a crate of six. This was indeed unusual, and because the shipment was insured, the airline reimbursed me. My only hope was that the thieves were familiar enough with Cockatiels to care for them properly—at least they knew enough to pick a male and female.

A friend of mine in the pet trade has told me that in his experience birds seem to withstand the rigors of shipping far better than fish, dogs, and other livestock. Tiny finches and the more delicate species might occasionally succumb if not in good condition, but we are concerned here with Cockatiels—very hearty birds, which are shipped as adults in good condition or young that have been thoroughly weaned from the parents (about ten to twelve weeks of age). Often birds will go off their feed for twenty-four to forty-eight hours following shipping, especially single birds that don't have other Cockatiels to emulate in the unfamiliar surroundings. Most birds can take this brief period of unfamiliarity and the resulting stress in stride if they are well-prepared physically.

TRANSPORTING BIRDS BY CAR. Many buyers may live within driving distance and would prefer to pick their birds up in person. This is nice, as the new owners can see the breeder's setup and can discuss at greater length the birds' customary care and diet—a good opportunity for both parties to learn from each other.

But how should the birds be transported? If the drive will only involve a few hours, it is both easier and safer to place the birds in a cardboard box with air holes and some seed. It is unlikely that the birds will eat much, if at all, as they will be upset by the strange situation. Water is unnecessary and will only spill. The birds in such an enclosure will not have much cause or room to panic and will not encounter any drafts. In their new home they will emerge frightened but physically unharmed.

For longer trips, a cage with perhaps a single perch, or none at all, may be considered (should the birds panic, they will not be injured by flying into or against the perches). If the trip entails an overnight stop, a perch can be carefully placed into the cage for roosting during the night. Provide water in an open dish. Seed and such should be placed on the floor. (Seed cups fitted into the cage should have been removed if they protrude in such a manner that they may be potentially harmful.)

The cage should definitely be covered with a light-colored blanket or towel, which will admit enough light should the birds want to eat but will exclude drafts and any sights that might cause fright. Again, in transit water will only spill; but greens, corn, or a slice of fruit will suffice if the birds need a bit of moisture before they arrive at their new home.

SHIPPING BY AIR. Shipping by air involves the same principles. Confine the birds in an enclosure devoid of things that might prove harmful to a frightened bird. However, there is more paperwork involved, and the enclosure must be suitable for shipping.

First, the breeder must know the customer's preferred airport for receiving the shipment, his address, and the telephone number where he can be reached at time of arrival, as well as his preference as to date and arrival time—if there is a choice in airline schedules (many people who are working during the day find it more convenient to pick the birds up late in the afternoon or evening). I recommend not shipping on weekends, as often there is only a skeleton crew at the air-cargo office, or none at all. Also, should there be an error in shipment, the birds might sit until Monday before they are correctly routed.

With the above information at hand, one should call the airline's air-cargo-and-freight telephone number. Do not contact passenger information, as they may not be aware that certain planes do not take live cargo nor that a minimum time of three hours leeway is needed if there s a change of planes involved en route. They also do not have the information at hand regarding the various state regulations on psittacine birds. Some states require a veterinarian's certificate verifying that the birds are in good health. This paper must be obtained within twenty-four hours of shipping and must accompany the birds.

It is best to schedule a direct flight. Should the airline contacted not have one, they are usually pretty good about referring you to another airline that does. However, sometimes a change in planes is necessary. This means that the birds must sit three hours between arrival and departure on the next flight, thus allowing their proper and prompt placement on the second plane. It is best that both flights involve the same airline. However, this is not always possible, and then the charge is usually almost doubled. Charges are figured by total weight of shipment. Fortunately, birds are lightweights, and it costs no more to send many birds at minimum weight than to ship one.

After obtaining the scheduling possibilities, contact the customer and confirm a date, with the understanding (and courtesy) that should anything arise (adverse weather, illness, etc.), you will contact them, or they you.

Twenty-four hours before shipping, call the airline and reserve the appropriate space. If shipping on a Monday, call the preceding Friday. It is best that the airline make out the air bill over the phone at this time to eliminate a possible last-minute rush when you arrive. You must supply both your and the receiver's names, addresses, and telephone numbers, the number and kinds of birds (Cockatiel), and be sure to mention the amount for which the birds should be insured. Ask for the air-bill number for reference, should the shipment be delayed and need tracing. (This is a possibility, not a probability.) If you will be calling the customer at this point, give him the air-bill number also.

The airline will request that you have the birds at the airport (air-cargo office, not the passenger area) at least 1½ hours before departure. Some airports require even more time. Allow for a possible traffic jam or a busy time in the cargo office, etc. They will weigh the crate of birds, and you will sign the forms after making sure all information is accurate. Usually shipments are sent collect.

The birds are now whisked away, probably never to be seen by you again. And you (if you're like me) will drive home rather sad, but hoping that the birds are going to as good a home as they left.

THE SHIPPING CRATE. The container in which the birds are shipped must be carefully designed. While parrots must have the box completely lined with wire, Cockatiels can be shipped in a sturdy corrugated cardboard carton, without fear of their chewing their way to freedom. If you are handy, quarter-inch plywood can be used to make a substantial shipping box. Remember that size-wise the birds should be confined to a degree, as they will be nervous and should not be allowed enough space to harm themselves if frightened. The height of the box should be no more than eight inches. The length and width are proportionate to the number of birds contained. The dimensions for one or a pair of Cockatiels might be 12″ × 9″. A 12″ × 24″ box can easily hold six birds.

Perches are unnecessary, and best not put in at all. A Cockatiel in a strange and small enclosure seems to prefer staying on the bottom anyway. A perch will only interfere with its movements and possibly cause injury.

The ideally constructed box is one that has a slanted window in one side. This way, if the airline crew packing cartons in the cargo area of the plane are short on space, there will be no chance that light and air will be cut off from the birds even if the box is tightly packed with other cartons. A box shaped like this is also less likely to be turned upside down. If a regular carton (straight on all sides) must be used, be sure there are small ventilation holes on all four sides.

The window opening should be covered with screening or wire mesh with no larger than ½″ by 1″ spacing—in other words, nothing that will allow a Cockatiel to stick its head through! Be sure there are no sharp wire ends protruding. In warm weather, the window should be made larger, or there should be two, on opposite sides of the crate. In cooler weather, make a smaller opening on only one side of the crate. The second window can be covered with plastic outside the screening or wire mesh to allow light and exclude drafts. On crates with a single window, burlap can be attached as a curtainlike flap that will admit some light and air but will insulate against chilling blasts.

All sides and the top of the box should be labeled Live Birds. This will help to encourage the cargo crew to handle with care and also to indicate right-side-up.

On the top of the box, write the name, address, and phone number of the person to whom the birds are being shipped and the airport of final destination. Your name, address, and telephone number may be printed smaller, in the upper left-hand corner. Please write this in indelible ink, in case it rains.

I have not mentioned water receptacles. If used, these may prove more harmful than beneficial in that the water will probably spill out and dampen not only the floor, but possibly the occupants as well, and thus make the birds more susceptible to colds. Cockatiels in the wild live in semi-arid or desertlike conditions. This adaptation persists in our captive-bred birds, so they are capable of surviving a day or more without water with no harmful effects. However, just in case, it is best to place in the box a slice'of apple, greens, corn, or the like.

A bountiful supply of seed should also be put into the box. Don't be stingy! If the birds have favorite treats such as millet sprays, these should also be offered to entice them to eat in transit.

A note should be enclosed in an envelope and taped to the box, giving all pertinent information: band number of each bird, date of hatching, variety of parents (Lutino, Pearl, Normal, etc.), diet and preferred treats, etc. This will help the buyer in identifying, breeding, and caring for the birds and aid in his record keeping.

After the birds are placed in the shipping container, be sure to use strong, waterproof tape to close it. There are plastic tapes as well as wire-reinforced paper tapes that are good and readily available. Please, no cellophane tape!

Wooden crates will be fastened with nails, screws, or wood staples, depending on the design.

PREPARING BIRDS FOR SHIPMENT. Birds to be sold should be given the same dietary extras as your breeders and future show birds. Their feathers should be maintained in top condition by frequent spraying.

The first thing a customer will be able to evaluate upon receiving his birds is their physical appearance. Feathers may get soiled or damaged in shipment, but most people can tell the difference between these recent accidents and plumage that was not in good condition prior to transit. These customers have paid good money for unseen birds, and it is not only a great disappointment to receive a humble package of ruffled feathers in return, but it damages the breeder's reputation. Any peculiarities of a particular bird should be stated openly to begin with (missing toe, bad habits or show faults, etc.) and price adjusted accordingly. The buyer will then be forewarned.

A week before shipping, the birds should be separated (if housed in large flights) and placed in quarters where the droppings and the birds' condition can be observed more closely. They should be given daily vitamins and extra nutritional treats to assure their coming through shipping in top condition, in spite of a few hours of trauma and perhaps a few days of adjusting to their new surroundings.

But ordinarily your birds should always be in such condition that they are ready to go any time! Even a week of concentrated effort will not condition a bird in questionable health. Conversely, a bird that has thrived on a continual good diet in a healthy environment will seldom be weakened by the stress of shipping. Be a responsible shipper—both for your sake, but most especially for your birds', who have no choice in the matter.

SHOWING

Purposes of Showing

Showing your Cockatiels is the best way to judge, through comparison with others' birds, just what you have achieved with your own. Someone who has only one pet Cockie need not feel he has no chance against a breeder who can pick and choose his best from many. Your tame Cockatiel might automatically sit up there fearlessly on the perch where it can be seen. A breeder can take a "wild" bird from his stock and, lacking a lot of work, the Cockie may huddle in a corner and panic with the judge's every movement. A bird could be the "Secretariat" of aviculture, but unless he struts his stuff, how will the judge ever know? A breeder must all but finger-tame his birds if they are to embody the goals he has reached through his breeding.

In other words, one's success in breeding does not necessarily mean success in showing. It takes a lot of work to consistently show successfully. If you win, you will never feel that your time was wasted. But if you lose because of some minor fault, like a perch placed too high or low, or the Cockie's claws were overgrown, it is entirely your fault and an unnecessary disappointment. If you honestly gave it your all, then you can sleep nights, knowing a better bird won, fair and square. And believe me, if two birds appear to be equal, the judge must resort to minor details to determine the winner. Don't let it be you who loses only because of something you overlooked or felt no one would notice! Showing your birds is work, but if you are going to do it at all, you might as well do a thorough job!

Shows are not only an incentive to furthering and upgrading the breeding of the species; they also serve to attract more fanciers to the field of aviculture. Enter to win! Bring only one or two of your best for each class. Be your own judge at home.

Don't just try to enlarge the class with mediocre birds. It is a waste of your preparation time and causes needless wear-and-tear on the extra birds. However, one should bench specimens of newer mutations that might not win against the older and more perfected colors, but take them with the thought that someone may never have seen a Fallow or Whiteface, or whatever. This is educational and a way to promote interest in the Cockatiel.

Showing is not a necessity but rather a nicety. Aside from personal education, one has a chance to meet many wonderful people. It has been proven to me that anyone who likes birds can't be all bad. Also, bird showing is not riddled with the politics that dog and horse shows have succumbed to. No handler (i.e., a professional involved to show the animal) is needed. In dog and horse shows, an experienced handler has an advantage over the novice, as he can cleverly hide faults or highlight good qualities in front of the judge. In bird shows, the birds alone are on display, and the judge has little idea which bird may belong to whom. Work your damnedest before the show, and the odds are that you will be a winner at the show.

At the Shows

The avicultural magazines carry announcements of the upcoming shows. Request a show catalog from the show or club secretary. Attending shows, talking to exhibitors, and visiting (or corresponding) with breeders will develop your eye for quality. The more birds you see, the better you can judge your own.

Shows run anywhere from one day's duration to four days, as with the National Cage Bird Exhibition and the Great American Bird Show, which are held in different sections of the country each year. If there is a lengthy trip involved, it may be best to arrive the day before, as judging usually starts early in the morning. There is a nominal entry fee for each bird. One registers by filling out an entry blank designating the Division, Section, and Class for each bird. Band numbers are also requested. You will then be given a numbered tag to attach to the front of the show cage. Each tag will have space for you to enter the variety of bird (Section and Class), band number, and your name and address. The tag must then be folded and stapled closed so that your name will not be visible until after the judging, when it may be reopened. This tag is then tied to the second-to-last vertical wire on the lower left hand side of the cage.

Since my first years of showing, the increased interest and support for Cockatiels have fortunately taken the species out of the hookbill category into a division of its own. The Cockatiel Division is divided into Sections: Normals, Pieds, and cross-mutations; Lutinos and cross-mutations; Pearls and cross-mutations; Cinnamons and Rare Varieties (Whitefaces, Albinos, Silvers, Fallows, and cross-mutations of these). Class level distinguishes cocks and hens: one class each for young (unflighted) hens and cocks (must be closed banded) and for older hens and cocks.

Judging begins at the class level with ribbons for first, second, third, and sometimes fourth places. The resulting placements in each class are then regrouped before the judge to be awarded First, Second, Third, and Fourth Best in Section. Eventually, section winners are again placed on the show bench for the Best in Cockatiel Division judging. Depending on the number of entries, winners can place from First through Tenth "Best in Show."

Realize that a judge can decide that a bird that placed second or third in one class (or section) is better than a first-place bird of another class (or section). A given class or section may be very strong in quality. It is not uncommon that a bird that won in its section does not even place on the top-ten division bench due to superior competition from other sections. At this writing, to have a Rare Variety bird placing in division is relatively uncommon, simply because these mutations have not had the time to build the quality necessary to compete with the more established mutations.

Often an Unflighted Trophy may be offered. *Unflighted* refers to a young bird closed banded within the present year. The band will be stamped with the current year and preferably bought and registered through a club, such as A.C.S., so that verification is easy. Registered bands also enable a bird's exhibition wins to be recorded towards Champion and Grand Champion points. Any bird, young or old, with an open band, or none at all, is automatically considered an adult bird, and so must be entered in an old class and is ineligible for the Unflighted Trophy.

It is also an invaluable experience if you can be a steward (or secretary) for a show. Stewarding entails assisting the judge and his secretary while judging is going on. You are expected to set up on the judging stand all the entries for each class, and then affixing appropriate ribbons at the judge's direction. If your judge does some thinking out loud, you will learn what he looks for or discredits. This is a college course in itself. However, watch your mouth. While working, the judge must never know whose bird is whose. Once all the judging is finished, you may ask the judge for a critique of your birds—both good points and bad.

Be sure to bring extra food and possibly your own water for the birds. (Sometimes the local water can cause a digestive upset.) Also, a small spray bottle, used for bathing, might be needed for a possible touch-up, as well as extra floor covering for the cages. The exhibition hall is hectic and remains open quite late at night. You may want to take something to cover the cages so that the birds will have more privacy to rest.

The majority of bird shows are held in the fall and early winter after the birds have molted and feathers are in spanking-new condition. Some clubs also hold what is called a "baby show" in the early summer to display each breeder's best young to date.

Breeders start thinking about shows as soon as their birds' eggs start hatching. We hope to recognize the pick of the litter and keep them for ourselves. This is hard, as what looks good at eight weeks may not prove the best at show time or even when breeding season rolls around.

You must discipline yourself to choose without emotion. For instance, you may be particularly fond of a pet or a youngster you struggled to hand-feed. While the bird might be easier to train to a show cage, its confirmation and condition may not be better than some "wild" youngster from your flight. The judge will not know that your personal favorite is on a first-name basis with the family cat, loves pizza (horrors!), and can recite the Fifth Amendment to the Constitution.

I also hesitate to take any of my best breeders. Should the stress of show training and the show itself set the bird back health-wise, you will no longer have your best to produce quality young. I don't mean to imply that all show birds automatically become basket cases because of the ordeal. I have never had a casualty, much less an illness, following a show. But show training and the show itself does stress the bird (not to mention the owner). Don't take too big a chance. If you have just bred the first purple Cockatiel, keep it safe at home and take its offspring next year. No trophy is worth the chance of losing an irreplaceable bird.

Early Preparation for Showing

About two months before show time, you must finally decide which birds are best and will be ready in time. Disqualify birds that have not at least started their molt; chances are, by show time they will either sport half-grown flight feathers or may be missing them completely. The stress of showing a bird still in molt could be detrimental to its health.

The following is a timetable for feather growth: three to four weeks for body feathers; four to five weeks for tail and wing flights and crest; seven to eight weeks for the two long, central tail feathers. Therefore, eight weeks before the show, scrutinize the bird's longest flight feathers. Differentiate between broken or cracked shafts and merely bent or fretted feathers. The latter can be rectified by washing or steaming; the former must be pulled and allowed the necessary time to grow.

Pulling feathers should not be done indiscriminately. There is a rare chance of damaging the feather follicle if it is done incorrectly, and growing new feathers is a small drain on the bird's energy. It is not particularly painful to the bird, much like pulling a few hairs from your head. However, a few rules are in order. With the bird securely in your gloved hand or a towel and your fingers holding the flesh just beyond the quill of the damaged feather, pull with a quick but gentle tug in the direction that the feather grows: straight out, not at an angle. Perhaps you would rather practice first on a non-show bird. Certainly it is not a difficult feat, but one can be nervous the first time.

Preparing a Lutino for showing takes a little extra effort. I place my best in a cage or small flight by herself about a month before the show. Thus the vulnerable thin spot on her head can be refeathered without the chance of an overzealous preening by some companion bird. (I say "her," as females seem less prone to baldness and therefore usually make better show birds.)

A good four weeks before show time, check and trim any overgrown claws. This will allow the clipped claws to round off through wear, so that they will look natural when gripping the perch, not freshly chopped. If cut nearer to show time, an emery board can be used to smooth them presentably. When clipping claws, be careful not to cut too close, as birds have a blood vessel running partway into the claw. On Lutinos, Cinnamons, and some Pieds, this is easy to see, but on most dark-clawed Cockatiels, one must make an estimation. It is best to clip a tiny bit at a time. To stop any possible bleeding, have one or more of the following on hand before

A Normal male Cockatiel together with a Lutino hen. Photo by Nancy A. Reed.

you start: Kwik-Stop, styptic pencil, alum, flour, tincture of benzoin, or a silver-nitrate stick.

GOOD SPORTSMANSHIP. If you have taken care of all the details to give each bird its fair chance to show its full potential, then you can honestly say on show day, "I have done my best!" Hopefully, thanks to your best efforts, the bird you have chosen does prove to be the best. If so, congratulations! Accept success with pride, but more importantly with humility. In another show, another bird may have you eating your hat. If defeated, accept defeat tactfully—no sour grapes! After the show, yes, the winner is hailed, and a graceful loser is respected, but a sore loser is so labeled.

SHOW TRAINING. Training a bird to a show cage is in reality teaching a Cockatiel the art of being inactive. Your goal is a bird that sits calmly on its perch and will not panic when either the cage itself is moved or the judge scrutinizes or manipulates the bird.

The show cage is minimal in size, so there is no room for adequate exercise. This is strictly a temporary situation that the Cockie must not be left in for too long a period of time, as it may become permanently inactive, which would be detrimental to the bird's health and definitely to future breeding success. Chances are, if the bird is good enough to show, you will obviously be thinking of using him or her for breeding. The bird must be given exercise periodically and allowed to catch up on its feeding if it has been picky in the show cage.

EARLY TRAINING. Show training can begin with nestlings, for handling the babies daily will instill a degree of steadiness. Granted, you will not know which bird will grow into a show bird, so handle all of them as often and for as long a time as possible. Even if all do not develop show potential, each will be steadier as a result and easier to tame, either for pets or as breeders for someone else. This is by no means a waste of your time, as a steadier bird is a better bird. Hand-feeding is ideal but not mandatory. Granted, once a baby leaves the nest box and is weaned in a flight, it becomes wilder, but when caught up it will calm down more quickly than one that was untouched by human hands as a baby.

Canary and Budgie breeders attach show cages to the flights or cages long before show time, enabling the birds to hop in and out and thus gradually become familiar with the show cage. With Cockatiels this is a bit harder to do, as show cages are markedly larger and heavier. If you can somehow accomplish such an arrangement, all the better. Cockies are curious by nature and will soon investigate the new quarters, becoming familiar with the show cage by choice rather than by force. Placing favorite tidbits such as millet sprays in the attached show cage will further entice the birds to enter. Usually, however, one must simply catch up a bird, place it in the cage, and start from this point.

Close To Show Time. Having picked out the best birds eight weeks before show time and pulled any damaged feathers, I find that, on the average, three weeks of training is necessary. Some birds are naturals, others are stubborn and take more time. Catch up the bird and place it in the show cage. Be it a pet or a "wild" Cockie, it will immediately object to the confined space, either by pacing back and forth like a Bengal tiger in the zoo, climbing the front bars, or sulking in a back corner—anything but sitting proudly on the perch. At the start, most birds will eat sparingly or not at all, so entice it with its favorites. Depending how much of a fuss the bird puts up, keep the Cockie in the show cage for twelve to twenty-four hours initially. If the bird paces for hours on end, cover the cage with a towel. Pets are most apt to do this, begging to get out, especially if they can see you. It is hard to say no. After this introductory period, return the bird to its regular flight or cage for one or two days for a breather, or allow a pet flight time.

Now gradually increase the time spent in the show cage, building up to the duration of the show. If the Cockatiel is

Above: Wing-pit sexing is reliable about 80% of the time. The yellow feather edging suggests that the Cinnamon youngster in the photo above is a female. Young males usually show no yellow, as in the photo below. Photos by Mark Runnals. **Facing page:** A Lutino in poor feather condition, which could be improved in a week or two by spraying with water daily. Photo by Horst Bielfeld.

not a pet, this means catching the bird each time by hand or with a net. Thus there is always a chance of a feather being damaged, which is a necessary risk.

FEEDING. Watch for seed husks in the show cages. If a bird refuses to eat for too long a spell, put him back in familiar territory. Do not let him get completely run down! A strong, healthy bird (your probable choice for showing anyway) can go a good twenty-four to thirty-six hours without eating with no harm done. Its exercise has been drastically limited, so its food intake can be minimal. Conversely, a bird that adjusts easily to the situation and eats like a vulture should have food rationed to the extent that it will not become too fat. In this case, millet sprays, too much sunflower, oat groats, hemp, or other fattening foods must be curtailed. Don't feed any food that may stain the feathers—no strawberries, etc.

A lean bird can be fattened up while being trained to its show cage. Give it all the goodies; with exercise limited, it can fill out quite nicely by show time.

Situation Training

Most judges use a "show stick." This is a pointer which enables the judge to move a Cockatiel around so that he can see the bird from all angles. For training, use a pencil, knitting needle, etc., as a judge might. I use an old telescoping TV antenna, a chopstick, or a drumstick. Tap on the bars, or touch the bird itself. The aim is to have the bird change positions without panicking. Again, a bird that can be scrutinized completely can be judged to its fullest potential. I've seen birds familiar enough with the stick to grab hold and have a tug of war with the judge!

Once the bird has become accustomed to its new accommodations, place the cage in an area of activity in the house. The more people who can pass by and stare at the bird, the better. You alone may not be enough, as it will get used to you but may panic if a new face confronts it. Also place the cage at different levels, (on the show bench it may be on the bottom, middle, or top shelf). In short, get the bird accustomed to all sorts of situations and people. If he is moved around and becomes used to a variety of people and places, you will have a well-trained show bird. Have other people handle the cage, talk, cough, or anything you can think of that the bird may encounter at the show. It will only be given a few minutes on the show bench, so don't let your weeks or months of patient work be wasted by an event you didn't anticipate.

CLEANLINESS. I have yet to see a top winner in a shaggy cage or box! I have seen many potentially good birds lose only because of their caging. If you have a Rembrandt, don't show it in a plywood frame! I cannot emphasize this enough! Why spend a lot of time and money raising superior birds, only to wreck their chances at the shows by showing them in dirty and chipped show cages? Immaculate cages and good training can be as important as the perfection of the breeding and condition of the bird. If two birds are of equal quality and steadiness, the judge may have no recourse but to consider the cleanliness of the cages as the determining factor.

The weeks before show time can be hectic enough with training and conditioning the birds. Show boxes should be repainted or washed and scoured at any slack period during the year and set aside in readiness. Anticlimactic as it may seem, as soon after the shows as possible, the cages should be at least washed and any droppings removed, as painted areas may become stained if left to sit a year. This may save you a paint job before the next show season.

BATHING. It is not usually necessary to bathe a Cockatiel. However, for show purposes, the long tail or wing feathers sometimes must be washed, especially on those birds that have white or yellow flights (Lutinos, heavy Pieds, female and young Pearls). These may have become noticeably dingy from newsprint or other floor coverings. Birds kept in smaller cages are more often in need of a bath than birds in

Above: A nice Albino Cockatiel. Photo by John P. Donahue. **Facing page, above:** The author's Pearl Cockatiel was Best in Show at the 1980 New Hampshire Cage Bird Association exhibition. Photo by Gary Lilienthal. **Below:** A Lutino pair. Photo by Nancy A. Reed.

flights, as the former spend more time in contact with the floor. Rarely does the whole bird need to be washed. Bathe the tail, or whatever, at least a week before the show, so that the natural oils on the feathers have time to be replaced. But don't bathe the bird just before introducing it to the show cage for the first time. Both events are traumatic enough without compounding the ordeal.

Hopefully, a bath will not be necessary at all. A light spraying or misting every few days while in the show cage will usually be enough to tighten the feathers and will induce the bird to preen, thus oiling and conditioning the feathers sufficiently itself. (Don't spray the seed! Remove the containers first. If you have seed on the floor of the cage, protect it with paper toweling.) When the water runs off the feathers as off a duck's back, you will know its feathers are in prime condition. An old spray bottle that has been thoroughly washed and rinsed, or a plant mister, is good. The finer the spray, the better.

Bent tail feathers can be straightened by dipping them in hot water or holding them over steam. Obviously, you must protect the bird's body from the heat of either the water or the steam, treating just the feathers.

Have all bath equipment ready so that the bird will not have to be subjected to the ordeal any longer than necessary. Baby shampoo is preferred, especially if any work is to be done around the head. Use a small piece of cloth or a soft brush for scrubbing, and have the water in the sink running warm into a bowl. Tissues or a dry, absorbent towel should be in readiness for drying. Next, pour a bit of shampoo on the counter and catch up the bird. Because the Cockatiel will not be too pleased with this and will express its displeasure by biting, cover the bird with a towel, exposing only the area to be washed. Expose the tail (the most usual soiled area) and place it in the puddle of soap. Dampen a square of cloth or the brush and scrub gently, following the "lay" of the feather, not against the grain, working up a lather. When clean, pick up the bird (in the towel) and immerse the soapy feathers in the bowl while water from the faucet further rinses the area. Make sure all the shampoo is out. Then dry with tissues or toweling and return the bird to a large cage or flight which will allow ample room for preening. This entire process should be accomplished as quickly as possible, as you have a pretty unhappy bird in hand. Do not place newspaper or the like on the floor of the cage between bath and show time; use paper toweling, wood shavings, or something that will not soil the feathers.

When washing an area of the body or the whole bird, work in a minimal amount of soap and rinse either by dabbing with a wet cloth or by very carefully immersing in warm water. Drying body feathers is more critical than tail or wing flights. Wrap the bird in a fresh dry towel to absorb as much moisture as possible. The bird may be left covered in the towel for awhile (secure, but keep the towel loose over its head so it can breathe). Following this, it may then be placed in a warm hospital cage or blown dry with a hair dryer. Usually the latter is practical only with a tame bird. Be careful not to burn its tender skin! The object is to get the bird as dry as possible, as quickly as possible.

In summary, bathe a bird only when really necessary. Tail feathers are the most usually soiled area and, fortunately, also the easiest and safest part of the bird to wash. Do not indiscriminately bathe the whole bird. The only time I have resorted to this was with a hand-fed baby that had been "glued" up with formula. Being tame, it could endure the ordeal better. Remember that you always take a chance of chilling the Cockatiel when you artificially bathe it, so precautions must be taken.

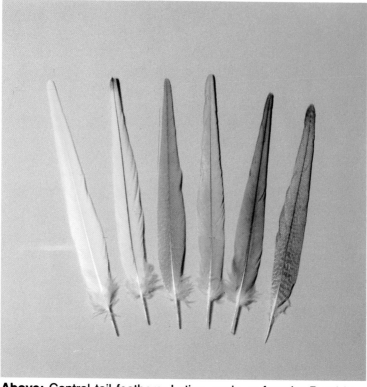

Above: Central tail feathers: Lutino, male or female; Pearl hen; Cinnamon hen; Cinnamon male; Normal male; Normal hen. Photo by Nancy A. Reed.

Facing page: A Cinnamon Pearl hen. The light area on the head derives from the Pied factor. Photo by Horst Bielfeld.

237

THE AMERICAN COCKATIEL SOCIETY SHOW STANDARD

(Updated 1985)

General Conformation

The Cockatiel is a long bird, with graceful proportions but of good substance (full bodied). From the top of the shoulder curve to the tip of the wing, from the top of the skull to the vent, and from the vent to the tip of the tail (ideally) should measure 7". The goal being a 14" bird with a 3" crest. The total bird being 17".

CREST: Should be long (goal 3"), with good density, curving from the top of the cere, fanning out to give fullness.

HEAD: Should be large and well rounded with no flat spot on top or back of the skull. Baldness will be faulted according to the degree of severity in each bird on the show bench. Our aim is for no bald spot, even in Lutinos. The eyes should be large, bright, and alert, and placed at mid-point between front and back of the skull. The brow should be well pronounced. When viewed from the front, the brow should protrude enough to indicate good breadth between the eyes. The beak should be clean, of normal length, and tucked in so the lower mandible is partially visible. Cheek patches should be uniformly rounded, well defined (no bleeding), and brightly colored (especially on males). Adult male Cockatiels will have a bright, clear, yellow head, sharply defined where the yellow meets the border of the main body feathers. A deep bib is preferred. There should be no evidence of pinfeathers.

NECK: Should be relatively long, have a very slight curvature above the shoulder and have a small nip above the chest area, giving the bird a graceful outline and eliminating the appearance of a "bull" neck or the "ramrod" posture of some psit-

The Ideal Cockatiel, drawn for the American Cockatiel Society in 1978 by Dr. Walter LaVoy.

Above: Lateral tail feathers: Lutino hen (barring inked for emphasis; a male would show no barring); Cinnamon hen; Cinnamon male; Normal male; Normal hen; Pearl (two variants). The amount of barring is variable. Photo by Nancy A. Reed.

Facing page: Flared tail feathers on a Pearl Pied Cockatiel. Photo by Nancy Richmond.

tacine species. An exaggerated "snake" neck would be reason for fault.

BODY: The body of the Cockatiel when viewed strictly from the side can be somewhat deceptive, as only a well-rounded outline of the chest will indicate whether the specimen has good substance. A frontal (or back) view shows more truly the great breadth through the chest (and shoulder) areas of an adult Cockatiel (more prevalent in hens). It is the strong muscular development that enables the Cockatiel to be such a strong flier. A Cockatiel should have a high, broad, full chest (more prevalent in hens); a slender, tapering abdomen; a wide, straight back (no hump or sway); and be a large, sleek bird.

WINGS: Should be large, wide, and long, enveloping most of the body when viewed from the side. Should be held tightly to the body, tips close to the tail with no drooping of the shoulders or crossing of the wings. The wing patch should be wide (goal of ¾″ at the widest point), well defined, and clear of darker feathers. All flight feathers should be in evidence. Covert feathers should illustrate their growth pattern clearly.

LEGS AND FEET: Should hold the bird erect at approximately 70° off the horizontal. Must grasp the perch firmly (two toes forward and two back), be clean, and claws not overgrown or missing.

TAIL: The longest flights should be the extension of an imaginary line straight through the center of the bird's body. A humped back will cause the tail to sag too low, and a "swayed" back might elevate the tail higher than desired. The feathers themselves should be straight, clean, and neither frayed, split, nor otherwise out of line. All flights should be in evidence.

Condition

A bird in top condition has clean, tight feathers: no frayed or missing feathers, no half-grown or pin feathers. The beak and claws must be of suitable length. There should be no unnatural roughness or scaling on the cere, beak, legs, or feet. If the bird is in good condition, it will be almost impossible to get it wet. Water will roll off like it does off a duck.

Deportment

In a good show stance, a Cockatiel should indicate a central line approximately 70° off the horizontal. It will present and display well on the perch.

Classification of Types

The following categories concern specific coloration aspects of the Normal and mutant Cockatiels. While definition is necessary for each type, it is to be remembered that coloration is not emphasized on the show bench as much as it may appear to be in the written Standard (see the Point Standard).

NORMALS: The color should be a dark gray, ideally uniform in color throughtout.

PIEDS: The ideal Pied will be 75% yellow and 25% dark gray. The goal being yellow pied markings over white pied markings. The aim being for tail and wing flights to be totally clear. The mask area should be clear, with no gray to create a "dirty" effect. Symmetry of pied markings is ideal.

LUTINOS: Ideally a rich, deep buttercup yellow throughout. Long tail feathers and primary flights will not be severely faulted for being a lighter shade of yellow than the body.

PEARL HENS: Extensive "heavy" pearl markings that are well defined, uniform, and without splotching. Ideally the pearl markings will be a deep buttercup yellow.

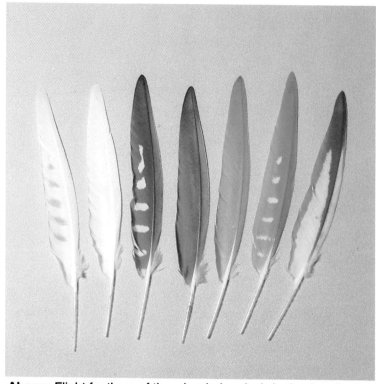

Above: Flight feathers of the wing (primaries): Lutino hen (yellow spots emphasized with ink); Lutino male; Normal hen; Normal male; Cinnamon male; Cinnamon hen; Pearl hen. Photo by Nancy A. Reed.

Facing page: A Pearl Cockatiel. Because of the extensive yellow coloration, Pearls of this kind are sometimes referred to as Golden Pearls. Photo by Horst Bielfeld.

PEARL MALES: The same as for hens, with less emphasis placed on the pearl markings.

CINNAMONS: The color should be cinnamon, uniform in color throughout.

FALLOWS: The color should be light cinnamon with a yellow suffusion, uniform in color throughout. The eyes should be ruby or red.

SILVERS: The color should be a dull, metallic silver, uniform in color throughout. The eyes should be ruby or red.

WHITEFACE: Same as the Normal, but devoid of all lipo-chrome. The mask area of the cock will be pure white.

ALBINOS: Will be devoid of all lipochrome, a pure white bird with ruby or red eyes. Primaries and flight feathers will not be severely faulted for being an off-shade of white.

CROSS-MUTATIONS: Will be judged by combining the color standards for all mutations involved.

SPLITS: Markings on split birds will not be penalized, as these represent a genetic factor of birds split to Pied and are not a matter of faulty breeding. A bird showing split markings is split to Pied. It can be split to other mutations but will not show the split markings.

CONCLUSION: Dr. Walter LaVoy is sincerely thanked for drawing the Ideal Cockatiel for the A.C.S.

A.C.S. Show Cage

DIMENSIONS: 17" high, 18" wide, and 10" deep.

A show cage mostly in accord with the A.C.S. specifications, with two perches perpendicular to the front. Photo by Nancy A. Reed.

Left: Lutino. Photo by Isabelle Francais.

Facing page: With daily misting with water, the plumage of these Lutinos could easily be smoothed (brought into good condition). Photo by Horst Bielfeld.

Below: Lutino—a good example of the degree of whiteness possible in this color variety. Photo by Horst Bielfeld.

FRONT: Chrome, removable roll-top.

PERCHES: Two ¾" dowels perpendicular to front.

PAINT COLOR: Inside: light blue semi-gloss. Sherwin Williams color SW1214 "Skylight." Outside: High-gloss black.

FEED AND WATER: An appropriate seed mixture will cover the bottom of the cage (not to exceed 1" in depth). Outside waterers that can be removed easily before judging; or, Lustar 307-A cups (available at pet shops or through the ACS) placed permanently inside, to the right side of the righthand perch.

BANDS: Double-banded Cockatiels will not be permitted at A.C.S. Regional or Specialty Shows. All other shows are governed by the club having the show. Double-banded birds will be considered as untraceable, with no band number recorded on the A.C.S. Show Report; consequently, no Champion points will be awarded.
Exceptions to double banding are: (1) Cockatiels from states that require a Cockatiel be banded with a state band will not be considered double-banded, providing they are banded with a traceable band. (2) The Show Secretary shall verify the state-required band and mark the Show Report as such. The cage tag will be marked with "D.B." on the front upper left corner to indicate that the Cockatiel is also banded with a state band.

A.C.S. Point Standard

The A.C.S. Point Standard has been formulated strictly as a reference aid for both the judge and the exhibitor in choosing the best birds. At show time, all birds will be judged by the comparison method, using the Point Standard as a guide.

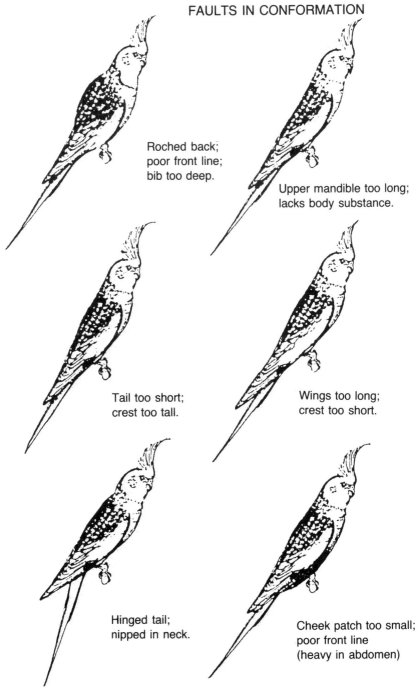

Roched back;
poor front line;
bib too deep.

Upper mandible too long;
lacks body substance.

Tail too short;
crest too tall.

Wings too long;
crest too short.

Hinged tail;
nipped in neck.

Cheek patch too small;
poor front line
(heavy in abdomen)

DRITTER PLATZ

Above: Third-place winner in a 1983 German competition. Photo by Horst Bielfeld.

Facing page: A male Whiteface Cockatiel. Photo by Horst Bielfeld.

Left: Lutino on a playground. Photo by Isabelle Francais.

CONFORMATION: *60 points*

SIZE: *20 points.* Overall length of bird (ideally 14″ not including the crest).

CREST: *10 points.* Length (ideally 3″) and density of equal importance.

BODY SUBSTANCE: *10 points.* Depth and breadth.

PROPORTIONS: *5 points.* Relationship of head size to body, to tail, to wings (ideally 7,7,7).

WING CARRIAGE: *5 points.* No drooping shoulders or crossed wing tips.

TAIL: *5 points.* All feathers fully grown and in place, clean and unfrayed.

HEAD: *5 points.* Large and well rounded. Eyes large, bright, and alert. Brow well pronounced. Beak clean, normal length, and tucked in. Cheek patches uniformly round and brightly colored. Bib deep.

CONDITION: *15 points.* Bird in obvious good health, tight feathered and immaculate.

DEPORTMENT: *10 points.* Steadiness and posture, basically the result of thorough show training.

COLOR AND MARKINGS: *10 points.* See the A.S.C. Show Standard for details under each type's classification.

UNIFORMITY OF COLOR: *5 points.* Uniformity in Normals, Lutinos, Cinnamons, Fallows, Silvers, Whitefaces, and Albinos. Markings on Pieds, Pearls, and cross-mutations.

DEPTH OF COLOR: *5 points.* Depth of color or degree of markings.

CAGING: *5 points.* All Cockatiels must be shown in A.C.S. Standard show cages when judged by A.C.S. Panel Judges. The cleanliness of these cages and general condition with respect to upkeep will be weighed by the judge.

INDEX

Page numbers in **boldface** refer to illustrations.